Praise for Linda Martella-Whi

"Linda Martella-Whitsett says some pretty audacious things: the mundane is as lofty as the spiritual, enlightenment is temporary, and GOD is not a deity. Her most audacious statement is also the richest and truest: you are Divine Identity. Got that! Read *Divine Audacity* and embrace the practices and you can't help but start showing up as who you really are–the light of the world."

—JANET CONNER, author of *Writing Down Your Soul* and *The Lotus and the Lily*

"Some people simply talk about the wonders of prayer while sharing stories about answered prayer. Linda actually teaches how to pray in a step-by-step, profoundly clear manner. This book will have you saying, 'Yes! This is what I have always sensed but had no words to express it.' Linda empowers us to realize our own True Identity, and then to claim it and live it."

—PAUL HASSELBECK, Dean of Spiritual Education and Enrichment, Unity Institute

"*How to Pray Without Talking to God* is required reading if you want to have a deeper connection with the Divine. Don't miss this wonderful book!"

—JOEL FOTINOS, author of *Think and Grow Rich Every Day* and *A Little Daily Wisdom*

"This book is a refreshing, inspiring approach to prayer that emphasizes one's connection with the Divine, however named, and the essential worthiness and goodness of all individuals. For those seeking a more meaningful connection with the Absolute, Martella-Whitsett is a wise guide."

—LARRY DOSSEY, MD, author of *Healing Words* and *Prayer Is Good Medicine*

"Linda Martella-Whitsett's *How to Pray Without Talking to God* gives clear and practical ways to apply the wisdom teachings in your day-to-day life. As you read, and more importantly practice, these timeless principles, you will begin to unleash your inherent spiritual power and ignite your divine potential."

> —JAMES E. TRAPP, president and CEO, Unity Worldwide Ministries

"This well-researched book belongs in the library of anyone who uses affirmative prayer as the basis of their prayer life; it will take your prayer life to the next level."

> —AUGUST GOLD, author of *The Prayer Chest, Prayer Partners,* and the children's book series Where Does God Live?

DIVINE
AUDACITY

DIVINE
AUDACITY

DARE TO BE THE LIGHT OF THE WORLD

linda martella-whitsett

HAMPTON ROADS

Cover design by Jim Warner
Interior designed by Maureen Forys, Happenstance Type-O-Rama
42 Powers image created by Rebeca Guajardo Davis

Hampton Roads Publishing Company, Inc.
Charlottesville, VA 22906
Distributed by Red Wheel/Weiser, llc
www.redwheelweiser.com

Sign up for our newsletter and special offers by going to
www.redwheelweiser.com/newsletter/.

ISBN: 978-1-57174-714-3

Library of Congress Cataloging-in-Publication Data available upon request.

Printed in Canada
MAR
10 9 8 7 6 5 4 3 2

Honoring my beloved husband Giles, my son Adrian, and my daughter Alicia. Life with you sustains me. You are the light of the world.

Awake, arise, and assert yourself, you dreamers of the world.
Your star is now in the ascendency.

—Napoleon Hill, *Think and Grow Rich*

CONTENTS

INTRODUCTION

ODDLY, I, A MINISTER SERVING a church community, have become less and less religious through the years. I would have expected otherwise; however, the more I have studied and meditated, the less I have relied upon religious constructs for my experience of the One Power, One Mind, GOD. Frankly, I have sworn off separation. We—the collective we—have perceived GOD to be an inaccessible superhuman, which locates GOD outside and beyond us. We have believed this GOD rewards and punishes, gives and takes away, requiring human suffering and sacrifice. We have thought ourselves to be unworthy of GOD; therefore, we are always striving but never succeeding to please a mostly disapproving GOD.

I propose that there is no such GOD.

My purpose is to transcend religion and to flatten spirituality, to level the field of thought and experience so that there is no higher and lower, no "more spiritual" and "less spiritual." I want that we realize our oneness with GOD. Instead of identifying ourselves as only human, I believe we free ourselves from our limited human perspective by identifying our nature as divine. I want that we revel in our Divine Identity! I want that we create our world and experience life from this realization. In a consciousness of only One, our conscious, intentional thoughts and actions arise from the One Power, One Mind, GOD. In this awareness, our mundane concerns become as spiritual as our lofty pursuits.

We have been convinced that we need to strive for divine approval, to earn our way into the heavenly kingdom. Post-religious teachings change the destination but retain the requirement: working toward enlightenment and learning our lessons. Consider, though, that our only-human striving for spiritual progress discounts the truth of our oneness with the One, the One that is the eternal, irrepressible, immutable All. GOD is all that, and we are one with GOD; therefore, moment by moment we are capable of being all that GOD is. Moment by moment, not by crawling and climbing, we are GOD living, loving, giving, and celebrating.

Enlightenment is temporary. It is moment by moment. Have you noticed that in one moment you can be totally connected, heart-centered, and free; but a moment later when a driver swerves her car into the parking spot you have been waiting for, you become . . . let's just say enlightenment comes and goes.

Practice makes moments of enlightenment more likely. Practice builds neural pathways that increase the likelihood of enlightened moments. Nevertheless, the most-practiced masters fall off the enlightenment wagon from time to time. Conversely, those who have had little or no education about their Divine Identity are known to have experienced sublime moments of awakened consciousness. Every one of us is capable of expressing, in any moment, something of the nature of GOD. Practice makes us more able. Practice makes progress.

Perfection is not the aim of practice. Athletes practice to build skill, and they must continue to practice in order to continue to excel in their sport. Injured basketball players rarely return to the game at peak performance after rehab; as they resume practice, their abilities resurface. They recall the mentality and posture cultivated through earlier periods of practice. Like athletes, we engage in spiritual practice in order to saturate our minds with the truth of our spiritual capacities. We build spiritual muscle to express our Divine Identity effectively, with increasing ease. With practice, we instinctively know what to think, say, or do to amplify the light of life, love, and all our spiritual capacities in any circumstance.

Any circumstance! Post-religious, New Thought teachings sometimes give the impression that we can get spiritual enough to eliminate all unwanted circumstances. This is not the purpose of spirituality, though. The greats—Jesus, Gandhi, Mandela, for example—never managed to eliminate unwanted circumstances. They were not exempt from human circumstances, and they did not promise us we could become exempt. Instead, they walked through unwanted circumstances as the light of the world, expressing from GOD, the One Mind. My intention is that we become so aware of our spiritual nature and capacities that we walk through unwanted circumstances in the same way we walk through *wanted* circumstances, shining the light all the while. Our Divine Identity can be our first resource rather than our last resort.

Within these pages, I intend to describe the indescribable GOD. In all places throughout the book, except in scriptural and other quotations, I use all capital letters for GOD to distinguish GOD, the One Mind, or Source, from the deity "God." I describe GOD according to twelve recognizable attributes, lights, or powers that are our capacities by virtue of our

oneness with GOD. Cultivating these capacities, we spiritual-
ize our lives in fulfillment of our divine purpose to be the light
of the world.

Although the twelve lights or powers are related and are,
in fact, various aspects of the One Mind, it is not necessary to
study them in order of their appearance in the book. One is not
a prerequisite for the next. I recommend studying one light or
power each week. Or, study one each month, focusing each of
the first three weeks on each of the three aspects of the power
and then integrating them during week four. Afterward, keep
the powers active by selecting one or two each morning to consciously practice throughout your day. Reread the corresponding pages, practice the meditations, and call forth your powers
during the circumstances of your day. You may want to set an
hourly alert as a reminder.

However you choose to approach *Divine Audacity*, may
your study and practice enrich your life. May you audaciously
shine the light of love, life, wisdom, and all spiritual powers
moment by moment, choice by choice.

Note: Unless otherwise noted, Bible verses are from the New
Revised Standard version. The Gospel of Thomas quotes are
translated by Stephen Patterson and Marvin Meyer (www.gno-
sis.org). The etymology of words in Bible passages are from
James Strong, *The New Strong's Exhaustive Concordance of the
Bible* (Nashville, TN: Thomas Nelson Publishers, 1990).

PART ONE
YOU ARE THE LIGHT OF THE WORLD

Arise, shine, for your light has come, and the glory of the Lord has risen upon you. For darkness shall cover the earth and thick darkness the peoples, but the Lord will arise upon you, and his glory will appear over you. Nations shall come to your light, and kings to the brightness of your dawn.

—Isaiah 60:1–3

IN DECEMBER 2012, KENYAN ABEL Mutai was about to win a cross-country race in Navarre, Spain. Just behind him ran Spanish athlete Ivan Fernandez Anaya, for whom a win would mean a place on the Spanish team for the European championships. Anaya was surprised when Mutai came to a stop ten meters short of winning, mistaking his stopping point for the finish line. Anaya caught up with his competitor and astonished onlookers when, instead of taking advantage of Mutai's mistake, Anaya guided Mutai forward to win the race.

Belleville, Michigan business owner Bob Thompson sold his road building company in July 1999. When the deal was done, he notified his 550 employees that they would share in the $428 million proceeds. Thompson gave hourly workers generous amounts, in many cases exceeding their annual pay. He presented salaried workers, who had no pensions, $1 to 2 million each in certificates available upon their retirements. To ensure they received the full million or more, he also paid the taxes on their windfalls. Bob's rationale? "I wanted to go out a winner and I wanted to go out doing the right thing."

Kyle Maynard has competed in wrestling and mixed martial arts, set records in weight lifting, and reached the summit of Mount Kilimanjaro—all without forearms and lower legs. Kyle was born with a congenital quadruple amputation. An inspiring author, athlete, and motivational speaker, Kyle encourages wounded warriors to stretch beyond physical limitations and achieve their goals. Kyle's mantra, and book title, is *No Excuses*.

Many years ago, a young woman, Chloe, was approaching death from the ravishing effects of multiple myeloma, cancer of the plasma cells within bone marrow. Chloe was in excruciating pain. As her minister, I visited Chloe hours before she died. I walked into her hospital room just as a few other friends were departing and a nurse was closing the blinds on the window next to Chloe's bed. I heard Chloe tell the nurse, in a whisper, "Please leave the blinds open." Overcome by the feeling of love and caring in the room, I said to Chloe, "How loved you are! This is your work right now, to let yourself be loved." Despite heavy medication and her body's agony, Chloe glowed like the sun and her eyes pierced my heart as she replied, "No. I am not here to be loved. I am here to be love."

Biographies of the greats—you know their names, Gandhi, King, Mother Teresa, Mandela—thrill us. Their relentless pursuit of justice and human dignity motivate us to treat others as equals. Their leaps over hurdles and their tenacity in the face of adversity stir us to be braver. Our larger-than-life heroes change the world. They display divine audacity. So did these four: Ivan Fernandez Anaya, Bob Thompson, Kyle Maynard, and Chloe, whose last name I do not recall.

What Is Divine Audacity?

Divine audacity is bold spiritual living, living under the radical premise that I AM divine. My nature is one with divine nature or GOD. I am able to boldly express the highest spiritual principles in the middle of everyday situations. I am courageously responsive. I am fearlessly self-reflective and self-corrective. I am intentional in large and small aims. I valiantly champion the goodness within myself and within each person I encounter. I hold myself accountable for thoughts, words, and actions that are in integrity with my Divine Identity. I dare to ignore the way things are and what cannot be done, bringing about the seemingly impossible. I suspend belief in the limitations that seem inherent in human existence to stretch beyond my known capacity. I disregard appearances to hold a vision of what *can be* so steadily that it must manifest. I overlook history, deriving my sense of direction instead from the source of life, love, and wisdom. I am not crushed by the weight of my commitments; rather, I passionately fulfill my sense of purpose. I uphold the world, all beings, and all intentions in the light of magnificent possibilities. I lift up rather than tear down. I believe in the inherent goodness of all people.

With divine audacity, I AM the light of the world, shining brightly. In my presence, others remember their Divine Identity. In my presence, others heal the illusion of separation. In my presence, others stand tall and behave humanely; they snap back from self-pity and self-derision to claim their spiritual capacities. In my presence, others sense, and act from, their essential goodness. In my presence, others come home to themselves, to the Self that is not their personality but their Divine Identity.

You don't have to be a superhero to express divine audacity. You don't have to be a superstar, or a super-anyone. You only have to attune to your essential nature, which is goodness, or GODness, and follow its lead in *all* things. Divine audacity is not reserved for life-or-death situations or singularly religious matters. Divine audacity is relevant in the nitty gritty situations we face every day.

Divine audacity is displayed by your open-hearted relative who dares to remain connected with you, reminding you of your inherent value when everyone else in your family has shunned you.

Divine audacity is displayed by the merciful parent of a murdered child who courageously asks for leniency in punishment of the offender.

Divine audacity is displayed by someone who wholeheartedly disagrees with another's point of view but champions the other's right to her viewpoint and seeks to understand.

Divine audacity is displayed by the aspiring musician who, knowing she stands little chance but that she *must* make music, auditions along with hundreds of contenders for twelve slots in the orchestra.

Divine audacity is uncommon valor in the midst of common human circumstances. The petite mother who lifts a 4,000-pound automobile to rescue her child pinned underneath it later exclaims, "I don't know where the strength came from, but it was the only way to save my child."

Engaging films and television shows portray characters navigating common human circumstances. Our fascination with them, I believe, stems from their relatability. The tension in such stories arises from a character's dilemma: Shall I behave honorably or dishonorably; shall I tell the truth or lie; shall I lift up or tear down?

A running story last season on the NBC show *Parenthood* involved Kristina Braverman's internal integrity struggles during her contest for public office. Kristina's opponent stooped to character denigration and innuendo. Kristina strove to take the high road, holding her tongue even though she could have revealed information that would have derailed her opponent's campaign. Kristina lost the election, but I imagine I was not the only viewer who sensed she was the real winner.

Divine audacity is fearless overcoming of only-human tendencies in order to do, or say, the right thing: that which unifies, harmonizes, strengthens, or uplifts. With divine audacity, you dare to be the light of the world.

What Does It Mean to Be the Light of the World?

"You are the light of the world." Jesus' audacious statement reveals a truth embedded within a metaphor common in his day that still remains applicable today. Let's examine *light* in Judeo-Christian tradition.

Metaphors about light, related to GOD and humanity, are prevalent in scriptures of every tradition. The ancient Hebrew word *owr*, translated "light," appears 123 times in the Hebrew scriptures constituting the Christian Old Testament, King James Version (KJV). In the New Testament, also KJV, the Greek work *phos* translated "light" appears 70 times. A few sentences into the first book of Genesis, we read that light was established by GOD, the source of light: "Then God said, 'Let there be light'; and there was light. And God saw that the light was good; and God separated the light from the darkness" (Genesis 1:3–4).

Although many Christian denominations interpret the Bible literally, Jewish tradition and modern scholarship explain that the characters, stories, statements, and chronicles contained in the Bible were not intended to portray historical accuracy or be taken literally. They were written by ancient Middle Eastern people for whom metaphor was a valid means of communicating truths. Therefore, we read of a God that acts much like a human, at times a superhuman. In this early account of creation, the Source, GOD, brings light into being.

In scripture, the literal meaning of light is conveyed in many passages, but in many others the word *light* is used figuratively. Light connotes a nonmaterial quality of being and conveys intelligence, consciousness, and understanding:

> The sun shall no longer be your light by day, nor
> for brightness shall the moon give light to you by
> night; but the Lord will be your everlasting light,
> and your God will be your glory (Isaiah 60:19).

> The Lord is my light and my salvation; whom shall
> I fear? (Psalms 27:1).

The Hebrew word for Jehovah, translated in these scriptures as Lord, means "the self-existent one." Think of Jehovah, or Lord, as the I AM or spiritual consciousness at the heart of you and me. The I AM is our Divine Identity, our unity with the Source. The I AM is our eternal beingness. This spiritual consciousness arose most notably in the character of Jesus, the central figure in the New Testament. Jesus is equated with GOD, with I AM, with light. Therefore, Jesus becomes known as the light of the world.

Stunningly, Jesus does not regard himself *alone* as the light. He acknowledges GOD is the origin of the light, the Father of Lights, and he recognizes himself as GOD's light. He also says to you and me:

> You are the light of the world. A city built on a hill cannot be hid. No one after lighting a lamp puts it under the bushel basket, but on the lamp stand, and it gives light to all in the house. In the same way, let your light shine before others, so that they may see your good works and give glory to your Father in heaven (Matthew 5:14–16).

In this radical statement of Jesus, revealing to you and to me that we have the same Christ nature as he, Jesus is astute about the science of light. Light is visually perceived radiant energy. Light makes the invisible visible; the unformed formed; the hidden revealed; the unknown known. Just as Jesus' life as the Christ, the anointed one, displayed visible evidence of his invisible Source, Jesus suggests that you and I, too, are anointed. Our light is from the Source, and we are capable of shining for all the world to see. Jesus further remarks, "As long as I am in the world, I am the light of the world" (John

9:5). Again, Jesus emphasizes that his purpose is to display visible evidence of the invisible Father, or Source, while living humanly.

Jesus' purpose in his day is your purpose and my purpose in ours. To be the light of the world, we plug into the Source, or One Mind, or GOD and derive from the Source our spiritual capacities that we express in common human circumstances. We attune to love, the power of unity, which leads in our conversation with a contentious coworker. We attune to strength, the power of tenacity, which pours forth from within us to persist in the face of seeming obstacles. We attune to imagination, the power of vision, which guides our hopes and dreams for the future.

Love, strength, and imagination are some of the innate spiritual capacities addressed in part two. But to be the light of the world, we must first acknowledge the light, admit the light, and allow the light.

Acknowledge the Light

Best-selling author Martha Beck once described a moment of profound spiritual awareness she experienced while undergoing a surgery. She saw a ball of light expanding to fill the space around her, explaining that she saw this in an otherworldly way beyond her material sense of sight. The light flowed into her body, saturating her and leaving her feeling "only the vivid, drenching, infinite presence of love and peace and joy" (*Leaving the Saints*, 102–3).

All That Is. Oneness. GOD. Divine Unity. Great Spirit. Source. One Mind. Whatever words we use to describe the indescribable power underlying life, this One is the source of light and our great resource. It is not a personality. It is a power. *The* power.

The Secret Book of John, aka The Apocryphon of John, is a noncanonical scripture found along with others in Nag Hammadi, Egypt, in 1945. Early in the text, John is enraptured with a vision of his teacher, Jesus, who is describing the One. In four hundred words of ecstatic poetry, John records a dazzling description of the indescribable One. In part:

> The One rules all.
> Nothing has authority over it.
> It is the God.
> It is Father of everything
> Holy One
> The invisible one over everything.
> It is uncontaminated
> Pure light no eye can bear to look within.
> The One is the Invisible Spirit.
> It is not right to think of it as a God or as like God.
> It is more than just God . . .
> It is absolutely complete and so needs nothing.
> It is utterly perfect
> Light . . .
> Light
> Producing light
> Life
> Producing life . . .
> ("The One," The Secret Book of John, 139–40)

Light is symbolic of divine illumination, the divine light we are by virtue of our oneness with the Source. Describing GOD as the source of light and acknowledging the light within us are resonant themes in religious writings of every tradition in every age. In Chandogya Upanishad 3:13:7, we learn "The light that shines above the heavens and above this world, the light that shines in the highest world, beyond which there are no others—that is the light that shines in the hearts of men" (Burke, "The Light Within").

Raised Roman Catholic, which I understood to be the only true religion, I was introduced to Buddhism in my eighth grade religion class. I found it fascinating, completely different from anything I had learned before, and plausible. It was the first time I ventured beyond what I had known about GOD and about myself, and I liked it. Another six years would pass before I was introduced to Ernestine, at age nineteen. Ernestine taught my aunt palmistry and other intuitive arts. I attended an ESP course with Ernestine, during which I experienced myself in past lives and developed a tentative trust of my intuition. I was nervous, however, because the kind of inner attunement Ernestine promoted was drastically at odds with my childhood faith.

One night, while driving home from a class session after dark, I was pondering whether this new endeavor was a good idea. Fervently I asked GOD, in my heart, if this training was good for me, and if it was for good, to show me a sign. Immediately—the thought had hardly formed in my mind—a shooting star (the first and only shooting star I have yet seen) dropped out of the sky and ran down my back. I felt a jolt of surging energy that landed at the base of my spine and then traveled back up into my heart. I was steeped in overwhelming joy and flooded with incomprehensible love. I had to pull my car over to the side of the road and stop.

That power was linked to me. I had called it forth. I realized, palpably, that the power beyond comprehension is within me; it is inexplicable yet real. It is my source.

Admit the Light

Chances are you can point to a few mystical moments of your own as indicators of your oneness with the Source. People tell me about their inexplicable, practically indescribable encounters, oftentimes confessing they had never before told anyone. They feared being misunderstood. I believe that visitations from saints and angels, physiological responses to Source energy, and phenomena experienced in response to our demand are not acts from a superhuman deity looking down upon us with pity or love. Rather, they are reminders of our innate power that is one with the One, or Source. Think about this: Your acute awareness of your ill friend's wholeness, your daring demand for clarity, or your pressing need for justice stirs the power within you. Your urgency broadcasts an SOS, but to whom or to what? If you believe in a deity that is separate and apart from you, you are likely to presume that this deity hears your prayers and answers by way of divine intervention. What kind of deity, though, would spare one human life but not another, or would rescue you from your crisis while allowing others to suffer?

When you conclude there is only one power, one Source, One Mind, you know you cannot be separate from the One. You recognize that your urgency broadcasts an SOS to you!

It says, "Wake up! Pay attention! See what is real!" In that instant, you break through the proverbial hundred thousand veils of illusion to the One Mind in which all things are possible.

Jesus' words, "What is impossible for mortals is possible for God" (Luke 18:27), call us to go beyond our human limitations in order to unify with the One Mind (GOD) in which we can do what Jesus did. We can heal the sick, feed the poor, walk on water, and change water into wine. Have we not witnessed seeming miracles, such as spontaneous remission of a cancerous mass? Have we not been thrilled to find something we thought was impossible actually become possible, which happened when my father who had disowned me returned and reclaimed me? Yet we dissociate ourselves from the One Mind and name it something other—a deity that brings about seeming miracles—instead of admitting the One Mind and I are one.

Admitting our Divine Identity can be challenging. Jesus was accused of blasphemy by religious judges, about to be stoned as punishment for claiming, "The Father and I are one." Referring to Psalm 82:6, Jesus exclaimed, "Is it not written in your law, 'I said, you are gods?'" (John 10:30; 34). Jesus died by crucifixion, which was the Roman punishment for insurrection. Jesus had dared to identify himself as divine, which in those days was the claim of Roman rulers.

In recent history, theologian, mystic, and former Catholic priest Matthew Fox was silenced and in 1995 dismissed from the Dominican Order amid the Vatican's attempts to excommunicate him for heresy. Among Fox's claims were that humans are born in original blessing rather than original sin and our nature is divine.

Pentecostal Bishop Carlton Pearson was declared a heretic by his denomination in 2004 for his self-described "expanded consciousness" leading to his inclusive spirituality. The subtitle of his 2010 book *God Is Not a Christian, Nor a Jew, Muslim, Hindu . . .* reveals Pearson's awakening to his Divine Identity: *God Dwells with Us, in Us, Around Us, as Us* (Atria Books, 2010).

A highly unpopular idea it is, in religious circles, to see GOD not as a person but as the One Mind or One Power at the heart of all that is and to identify ourselves as one with the One Power. As the above-mentioned religious leaders learned, traditional images of GOD as a superhuman deity and humans as unworthy sinners are broadly considered inviolable. Identifying ourselves with the Divine especially goes against religious convention. It threatens the institutions that have claimed to speak for GOD and have wielded power over us. We are labeled apostates, blasphemers, and heretics for admitting the truth that religious mystics through the ages have known and have been silenced for proclaiming.

Socially risky to admit publicly, our Divine Identity is equally problematic to admit to ourselves. If we accept that all we know about GOD is also true about ourselves, we must accept personal responsibility for our thoughts, words, and acts. We can no longer pretend helplessness in the face of human experience. Admitting our Divine Identity requires us to draw from, yield to, and express the One Power consciously, every day. We have to live from this realization. It requires audacity.

In his own culture, in his own way, Jesus seems to have admitted the truth he knew about GOD and himself, and about us. Although the originating texts were written generations after Jesus' lifetime, the following verses reflect the early Christian understanding of Jesus' message.

> *I am in you and you are in Me, and where you are, there I Am. I am sown in all things, and when you gather Me, it is you, yourself, who you gather (fragment from the Lost Gospel of Eve, Richard Hooper, Hymns to the Beloved).*

Interpreted literally by fourth-century orthodox church leader Epiphanius, this gnostic verse was associated with sexual intercourse. Mystics of all times have considered human sexual intimacy, or union, as a metaphor for spiritual unity of humanity with the Divine.

> *Jesus said to him, "I am the way, and the truth, and the life. No one comes to the Father except through me" (John 14:6).*

In this passage, Jesus is speaking from his Christ, or "I AM," nature and reminding us of ours. Throughout his teachings, Jesus proclaimed that we all have the same "Father" and therefore the same potential to realize the Christ or anointed consciousness. Each of us must rely upon our Christ or spiritual nature in order to experience our oneness with the Father, or Source.

> *Again Jesus spoke to them, saying, "I am the light of the world. Whoever follows me will never walk in darkness but will have the light of life" (John 8:12).*

Similarly, Jesus' Christ or spiritual nature reveals that the I AM or Christ nature is the light by which we become enlightened. The light of spiritual understanding is inherent, by virtue of our divine origin.

> Jesus said, "If they say to you, 'Where have you come from?,' say to them, 'We have come from the light, from the place where the light came into being by itself, established itself and appeared in their image.' If they say to you, 'Is it you?,' say, 'We are its children, and we are the chosen of the living father.' If they ask you, 'What is the evidence of your father in you?,' say to them, 'It is motion and rest'" (Thomas 50).

In this verse from the Gospel of Thomas, Jesus equates the Father or Source with light. In keeping with the first book of Genesis, the light comes from the Source and is reproduced within humanity. The light of spiritual understanding is our nature at all times, during wakefulness and when asleep, in activity and in stillness, embodied in physical form then formless after physical death.

> There is light within a person of light, and it shines on the whole world. If it does not shine, it is dark (Thomas 24b).

Jesus identifies the light of spiritual understanding not only within himself but broadly, in the universal "he." What good is the light, Jesus seems to say, if we do not shine? Failing to shine the light of spiritual understanding is living in the darkness of ignorance.

The words that I say to you I do not speak on my own; but the Father who dwells in me does his works. Believe me that I am in the Father and the Father is in me; but if you do not, then believe me because of the works themselves. Very truly, I tell you, the one who believes in me will also do the works that I do and, in fact, will do greater works than these (John 14:10–12).

Jesus admits that his authority comes from his attunement to the father, or Source. Like Jesus, when we are so attuned, we become indistinguishable from the Source. Our words and our actions radiate the light of the Source.

No matter how compelling our enlightened interpretations of scripture might be, and no matter how desperate humankind is for the message of oneness, most people either shy away from or reject outright the audacious claim of Divine Identity. Admitting this truth, for many, seems unthinkable because of religious dogma that separates GOD from humanity, naming GOD good and humanity sinful. Moreover, many misunderstand the Divine Identity. In the words of Father Richard Rohr, "Some will think I am arrogantly talking about being 'personally divine' . . . ." Rohr, explaining the True Self, or Divine Identity, writes:

> The discovery of our own divine DNA is the only, full, and final meaning of being human. The True Self is neither God nor human. The True Self is both at the same time, and both are a total gift (*Immortal Diamond*).

It's a challenging calling, to be the light of the world. We flinch in the thought that we would have to live too brightly all the time, never being fully human perhaps. But being the light of the world is nothing personal; it is the light of spiritual understanding that dawns within us all. Charles Fillmore, cofounder of the Unity movement, wrote:

> Everyone has within him the light of divine understanding. Those who do not recognize that they have this inner light are thinking intellectually instead of spiritually. The Christ light comes forth from God and under all circumstances is aware of its source (*Mysteries of John*, 86).

The inner light is the brightness of the One that harbors no sense of separation and lives in harmony. It is the consciousness that stands non-condemning and nonreactive, pausing to bring forward the illumination of the inner spirit. It's not about our small thoughts and feelings. It's not personal. It's universal:

> If ten lamps are present in one place
> each differs in form from another;
> yet you can't distinguish whose radiance is whose
> when you focus on the light.
> In the field of spirit there is no division;
> No individuals exist.
> (Mevlâna Jalâluddin Rumi)

Admit your Divine Identity. You do not have to beg a superhuman deity to confer it upon you. You do not have to earn it through penance and suffering. You do not have to go on a lifelong journey to find it, as if it were a treasure hidden elsewhere. You do not have to feign helplessness or behave with false modesty in order to feel acceptable in a culture that mistakes Divine Identity for egomania. You can rightfully claim your Divine Identity moment by moment, choice by choice. In biblical terms, you are a city built on a hill; your light cannot be hidden (Matthew 5:14).

Allow the Light

As Jesus did, we radiate the light of the Source when we are attuned. To be attuned to the Source is to be united with the Source, and to be united with the Source is to allow the light of the Source to shine. We allow the light of the Source in the frequently misunderstood spiritual activity of surrender.

Every faith tradition values surrender as a key to heightened spirituality. In Christianity, Jesus is regarded as a model of surrender by acquiescing to his brutal crucifixion. The Gospel writers, who had not witnessed Jesus' solitary agony in the Garden of Gethsemane, placed this plea in Jesus' mouth: "Father, if you are willing, remove this cup from me; yet, not my will but yours be done" (Luke 22:42). Early Christian leaders provided, by this prayer, a pattern for followers to accept hardships in their own lives.

Other statements accounted to Jesus have reinforced the idea of surrender as submission to the will of the deity: "Jesus said to them, 'Very truly, I tell you, the Son can do nothing on his own, but only what he sees the Father doing; for whatever the Father does, the Son does likewise'" (John 5:19). The teaching "I can do nothing on my own" has led to a view of humanity as helpless and broken, the remedy for which is reliance upon God. However, Jesus is claiming his spiritual authority in this statement, doing what the father does or understanding the nature of GOD and living accordingly.

Surrender, at its best, comprises two distinct actions: releasing only-human limitation and yielding to our spiritual nature or Divine Identity. Release is one of our spiritual capacities, our spiritual power of cleansing, renunciation, and repentance. We release the false notion of powerlessness, sinfulness, and any negative interpretations of ourselves, knowing that we are not merely human. We release the view of the limited or finite self operating from primitive impulses based upon insecurity and scarcity. In the words of spiritual teacher Michael Beckwith, ". . . surrender is freedom from the bondage of ego. We free ourselves from living in the neurotic consciousness of 'me, myself and I.'"

The second activity of surrender is yielding to our spiritual nature or Divine Identity. We give way for the wisdom of the Self to arise in our awareness. We understand that we do not yield to any external authority, including a religious leader or text; we go within, to the state of awareness of our essential unity with the Source, GOD.

Surrender, therefore, is not submission. To be clear, I find it helpful to substitute the word *allow* for surrender. In allowing, I understand that I am not giving up; instead, my finite self (my sense of myself as only human) is opening to the Infinite Self, also known in Christian metaphysics as Christ consciousness, or Divine Identity.

When we allow or surrender, we are releasing ourselves from held beliefs. We become open to the universal wisdom that has always been right here but was clouded by the beliefs of the limited or personal self. When we allow or surrender, we have access to all that we could not see or imagine before. Divine ideas that had always existed but had been unavailable to us in only-human consciousness now occur to us. We find creative solutions to challenges and seemingly miraculous turns of events in the state of allowing or surrender, for all possibilities exist in the One, and the Infinite Self is one with the One.

The key to allowing, for me, is to stop struggling. Once a young yogi who had been bathing in the Yamuna River was swept off his feet by the swiftly flowing current. Frantically flailing to stay afloat, he soon tired and was drowning. He turned his thoughts to his guru, and in that instant he heard his guru's voice saying, "Stop struggling. Lie down on your back." He did. He floated to shore.

Be the Light

It is impossible to see anything in the real realm
unless you become it.
Not so in the world. You see the sun without being
the sun,
See sky and earth but are not them.
This is the truth of the world.
In the other truth you are what you see.
If you see spirit, you are spirit.
If you look at the anointed, you are the anointed.
If you see the father, you will be the father.
In this world you see everything but yourself,
But there, you look at yourself and are what you see.
(Gospel of Philip, *The Gnostic Bible*, 270–74)

Being the light is our moment-by-moment, choice-by-choice agreement to act from a consciousness of unity with the One Mind. In spiritual understanding, "When you see the father, you will be the father" (Gospel of Philip). Being unified, rather than divided, we could be said to be in the kingdom consciousness, or heavenly state of being.

The heaven most commonly subscribed to is the quintessential afterlife reward, an eternal resting place. Heaven is often regarded similarly to the million-dollar prize on the long-running reality TV show *Survivor*—except that you must suffer through earthly trials and then *die* before earning your heavenly reward.

Interestingly, Jesus presents us with a heaven that is "at hand" or right in front of us (Matthew 4:17) and "within you/among you" (Luke 17:24). In the noncanonical Gospel of Thomas, Jesus bluntly states: "the kingdom is inside of you and it is outside of you" (Thomas 3).

These messages convey a totally different conceptualization of heaven than the theologically mandated afterlife resting place. The word *heaven*, translated from the word *Shem* in ancient Aramaic (Jesus' spoken language), is laden with various meanings, according to Aramaic scholar Neil Douglas-Klotz: the Source, that which rises and shines in space, light, sound, vibration, atmosphere, name—the entire sphere of being. Klotz says: "In this picture, we are part of a universe of vibration in which everything is connected as though by a wave of sound. When we realize this connection and this vibration, we are, so to speak, in heaven" (*Original Prayer*, 13).

Although many Bible scholars argue that the original Gospels would have been written in Aramaic, most of today's

English-language translations derive from the writings in Greek. The Greek word *ouranos*, translated into English as *heaven*, means "the sky." The heavenly state is metaphorically sky-like, an elevated state of being, an expansive heightened awareness. Heaven is a condition of consciousness, our awareness of enduring truth beyond passing circumstance; our knowing of strengths and capacities we would have never claimed in only-human consciousness; and our experience of unity with all that GOD is, with other beings, and with all of life. Being the light of the world is expressing our elevated, unified consciousness within the world around us moment by moment, choice by choice.

Being the light requires us to claim, audaciously, our Divine Identity or I AM power. In an elevated awareness, we understand that the source of the light is not personal, that I AM is not personal power. It is *spiritual* power. Just as GOD is not a personality, the Infinite Self, I AM, or Divine Identity is not our personality. The spiritual Self identified in Hindu scriptures with a capital *S* is the One Mind we express based upon our realization of its nature. Knowing our light derives from the One Mind or GOD and not from our personality, we can feel assured that we do not have to rely upon our human characteristics as our source. This is good news, right? We can be fully human, with our human inconsistencies, foibles, and incompetencies; even so, we can be the light of the world. Read about Moses in the Hebrew scriptures or Arjuna in the Bhagavad Gita for inspiration. Moses and Arjuna, along with many other characters in the writings of various faith traditions, demonstrate how to become visible expressions of the invisible light despite having human imperfections.

In the way that a prism bends light into an array of diverse colors, or a wintry cloud breaks out into billions of unique snowflakes, the inexpressible One takes on infinite expressions—as life, love, intelligence, and all qualities that could be recognized as divine. All these divine qualities are expressible by you and by me. We are the inexpressible One expressing. We are the light of the world.

Whenever we experience and express love, we are divine love. Whenever we intuitively know when to act and what to do, we are divine wisdom. Since the divine is not a person but a principle and we are, so to speak, a chip off the old block, the love principle and the wisdom principle are our true nature. We can identify ourselves as these principles. We can shine the light of these principles into our world.

In his book *One Mind*, Dr. Larry Dossey tells of Nobel Laureate and geneticist Barbara McClintock's uncanny capacity to have "a feeling for the organism" she studies. Dossey writes: "In order to experience 'a feeling for the organism', one has to dare to be the organism. This means going beyond the boundaries that separate us from one another and from other life forms. It means entering the One Mind" (202).

PART TWO
SHADES OF LIGHT—
OUR SPIRITUAL POWERS

CHRISTIAN METAPHYSICAL TEACHER and founder of the Unity movement Charles Fillmore approached the Bible as a spiritual story about our evolution from personal or finite being to divine or infinite being. Each character in the Bible represents an aspect of our own evolving being. Accordingly, Fillmore studied and meditated to understand the significance of Jesus' twelve disciples. He concluded that each of Jesus' disciples embodied a characteristic—a principle, a power—that well served Jesus' mission. True to his approach was Fillmore's interpretation of Jesus Christ as our spiritual nature, aka Divine Identity or infinite being; therefore each of the disciples represents one of our spiritual abilities that we call into service of our mission to be the light of the world.

Some of the disciples are easily linked with corresponding powers. For example, Simon Peter is widely associated with faith, as is John with love. Read for yourself Fillmore's groundbreaking book *The Twelve Powers*, first published by Unity as *The Twelve Powers of Man* in 1930, to learn more about Fillmore's association of each disciple with a particular spiritual ability.

My approach in the following chapters is not to repeat or report on the classic Unity teachings about the Twelve Powers, for I cannot improve upon them. Instead, my desire is to profile each power, describe some of its aspects, illustrate ways it can be expressed, and suggest practices to develop it as a useful spiritual power in daily living. Each power, or spiritual ability, is significant by itself, but, as is true for personality profiles such as the classic Myers-Briggs assessment, one attribute by itself does not define us. In fact, all our spiritual abilities are shades of the One Mind, and all of our spiritual abilities share these characteristics.

All Spiritual Abilities Share One Source

The source of all power is GOD. GOD is not a personality that gives us power but is the actual power itself. For example, GOD is not a personality that gives us love. GOD is love! GOD is the principle. One with GOD, we are the principle also, but with our capacity to act in the world we are expressers of the principle. Therefore, we can say about love: GOD is love. I love, loving.

> God does not love anybody or anything. God is the love in everybody and everything. God is love; man becomes loving by permitting that which God is to find expression in word and act (Charles Fillmore, *Jesus Christ Heals*, 27).

Likewise, GOD is faith, understanding, will, imagination, zeal, power, wisdom, strength, order, release, and life. GOD is faith. I AM faith, being faithful. And so on.

All Spiritual Abilities Are Inherent

All of our spiritual powers or abilities are inherent. Arising from the Source, we come fully loaded with every ability. Our abilities are native to us, not acquired, never subject to depletion, always existent.

Our spiritual abilities are invisible, vibratory, nonphysical energies that can be stimulated and sensed. Our physical body resonates with these energies. Similar to the chakras, seven energy centers recognized in Eastern medicine and spirituality, the twelve spiritual abilities I will describe can be stimulated by concentrating attention on their vibratory representations within our physical body. To locate each power's center, refer to the diagram on page 36 and to the meditations corresponding with each power.

All Spiritual Abilities Are Latent

Although our spiritual abilities are natural to us, they exist in potential until they are recognized, activated, and developed. From childhood forward, we have developed these abilities in their physical expressions. We have learned, for example, how to express wisdom as sound judgment when making decisions and how to express harmonizing love in our relationships.

Every one of our spiritual abilities has deeper and broader means of expression that, when developed under the direction of our Infinite Self or Divine Identity, produce potent effects in our lives, in our communities, and in the world. The Infinite Self, or the Christ—says Fillmore—must take the lead, rather than the personal self, often named the ego self. The personal self has only a short range of vision serving itself, whereas the Infinite Self is oneness knowing only oneness; therefore its action is for universal good.

All Spiritual Abilities Must Be Directed

The expression of each of our spiritual abilities is based upon the intelligence behind it. By itself, each ability is neutral; it can be called into service for help or for harm, to bless or to curse. Love, for example, can be expressed as obsession when I perceive myself to be an only-human blinded by passion, believing that a person—precisely *this* person—must be the antidote to my loneliness. In the same condition, loneliness, I can express the harmonizing power of love within myself to neutralize loneliness and display the love I AM by kind self-thought and acts of loving service that connect me with others.

The personal self is biologically oriented toward surviving. This does not make the personal self wrong or inferior. It makes the personal self limited in its scope of awareness. The personal self subscribes to worthy values such as intimacy—to love and be loved; physical, material, and financial well-being; and safety. The personal self is also capable of caring about the survival of others above or besides itself, as when a parent sacrifices his own ambitions for the sustenance of his family or joins a rescue team after a destructive hurricane.

The personal self longs to know itself as eternal and infinite. The personal self longs to pierce the border beyond which it senses its rightful domain referred to as the kingdom of the heavens or the field of oneness. The personal self longs for greatness. We look up to the inspirers in our world who shine light on our greatest capabilities. We are inspired by reminders to express love as harmonizing compassion not only to victims of crime but to the perpetrators as well, seeking to understand the suffering that prompts a person to violence. Inspirers are the prophets among us who, like Jesus and leaders in recent history—Gandhi, Mother Teresa, the Dalai Lama, Mandela— teach through their example how to express our abilities most nobly and to the good of all. To pay homage to these masters, however, is hollow unless we adopt their practice of seeking to express most nobly, most spiritually, our great abilities.

Our spiritual abilities, then, need training.

> When man is developing out of mere personal con-
> sciousness into spiritual consciousness, he begins
> to train deeper and larger powers; he sends his
> thought down into the inner centers of his organ-
> ism, and through his word quickens them to life.
> Where before his powers have worked in the per-
> sonal, now they begin to expand and work in the
> universal (Fillmore, *The Twelve Powers of Man*, 4).

Fillmore referred to this training as the work of regeneration, or transformation:

> Spiritual transformation of our love ability, for
> example . . . broadens, strengthens, and deepens
> it. We no longer confine love to family, friends,
> and personal relations, but expand it to include all
> things (Fillmore, *Christian Healing*, 134).

Regeneration or transformation occurs as we seek to understand universal truth, which comes through study, prayer/meditation, and reliance upon the Infinite Self for revelation of truth.

Consciousness Is Pivotal

Anita Moorjani, in her book *Dying to Be Me*, revealed truths she discovered through cancer and a near-death experience:

> The entire universe is alive and infused with consciousness, encompassing all of life and nature. Everything belongs to an infinite Whole. I was intricately, inseparably enmeshed with all of life. We're all facets of that unity—we're all One, and each of us has an effect on the collective Whole (Moorjani, *Dying to Be Me*, 70).

Anita experienced a further awareness during her near-death experience: that we are not *sometimes* human and *other times* spiritual but in fact are *always* spiritual. Sometimes we are aware of our spiritual nature, other times not.

Consciousness is awareness. It is awareness based as much on memory and unconsciously stored impressions as it is on experience in the moment. Consciousness is a worldview formed from our inner responses to all we have heard and seen, learned and practiced, lived and dreamed.

A common expression, "We are spiritual beings having a human experience," points to the truth of our eternal spiritual nature while explaining why we do not always recognize our true nature. In any moment, our awareness is of either our human/personal or our divine/spiritual identity, of our temporal or eternal nature, as a finite being or Infinite Self. Our awareness or consciousness is pivotal.

We can turn to the world around us or to the world within, where we access boundless power beyond the only-human capacity. We can be fed by our circumstances or by the Infinite Self. We have a choice, but when we view ourselves as only-human, it hardly seems a choice. In only-human consciousness, we do not have eyes to see the world within. This is why consciousness development is necessary: so that we know, first intellectually and then wholeheartedly, the reality of the Infinite Self. The finite or personal self, sometimes named the ego self, exists within the Infinite Self—there is no separation and no *other*. In times of earnest need, during peak experiences, as a fruit of sincere study, or unbidden, we may penetrate the perceived border of our personal self and glimpse the Infinite Self. How do we recognize the Infinite Self?

Realize the Infinite Self

We recognize the Infinite Self by its effects: our inner peacefulness, joyfulness, and well-being; our broader perspective of oneness existing beyond time and space; and giving of ourselves fully into life. We cultivate healthy, satisfying, and supportive relationships. Our service to others empowers them to recognize their own spiritual capacities. We deeply feel all of our human emotions without harboring any of them. We revel in the activity of today on the road to tomorrow. We treasure people who come into our lives and we lovingly release them when they depart. Our presence blesses others.

The personal self cares about itself. It cares about winning, about saving face, about getting ahead. The Infinite Self cares about none of this. The Infinite Self pours out its powers over all, like the rain that drenches everything in its path. Love unites. Life animates. Strength holds to the truth. Power acts with authority. Release eases. Imagination conceives.

At the June 2012 Ohio State Division III girls meet, high school distance runner Meghan Vogel observed opponent Arden McMath collapse twenty meters from the finish line. Meghan could easily have run past Arden, but she stopped, helped her to her feet, carried her toward the finish line, and placed herself behind Arden so that Arden finished first.

Another day in June 2012, Delroy Simmonds was waiting for the subway, on his way to a job interview, when he watched a gust of wind toss a baby in her stroller over the edge of the platform and onto the tracks. Without thinking, Delroy jumped down to the tracks and lifted the injured baby up to her mother followed by the stroller. An approaching train honked and came to a screeching halt just seconds before he climbed to safety. Delroy missed his job interview, but another employer who learned of his heroism offered him a position.

Arden McMath and Delroy Simmonds audaciously displayed their Divine Identity at times when they could have been all about themselves. Both of them said later what everyone says when rising above the interests of the personal self: It was the only thing to do.

When others are in need, when challenged by disease, when medical bills have drained the bank account, when your lover leaves—when times are tough, there is no better time to pivot in the direction of the Infinite Self. We can stand in the midst of human circumstances undaunted by them; putting on the mantle of divinity, so to speak, as we are willing to disregard frightening or troubling appearances—illness, death, lack, loneliness. We long to rise above our circumstances, pluck the jewel out of the muck, make something better out of the bad, and transform trouble into a blessing. The drive to be greater than human thoughts, feelings, and experiences is natural to us, because we are divine.

Whenever we feel tension between where we are and where we want to be, we are on the threshold of the Infinite Self. Whenever we feel torn between extending mercy and teaching someone a lesson, whenever we feel eager for change and yet daunted by the idea of it, whenever we feel angry toward another person while sensing our part in the drama, let this tension be our signal to choose a response from the Infinite Self.

Activating our spiritual abilities is a choice. Making the choice, then, how do we get equipped for expressing these abilities in a spiritual way? We *be*. We get into being through practices that foster beingness, such as meditation, journal writing, yoga, prayer partnership—any practices that call us out of human *doing* into our natural state of *being*: "Be still, and know that I AM God" (Psalm 46:10).

The effort required to pivot in the direction of the Infinite Self is, paradoxically, non-effort or effortless effort—a clue to which exists within the common label for our species: human *being*. An only-human consciousness is focused on *doing* rather than *being*. *Being* is the spiritualized state of awareness in which we realize our Divine Identity. Whenever I shift attention from my personal self toward the Infinite Self that is GOD, which is the *real* Self, I become what GOD is. I turn within to *be* love, strength, wisdom, life, and all spiritual capacities.

Another practice to activate spiritual abilities is affirmation. In the words of Charles Fillmore,

> We grow to be like that which we idealize. Affirming or naming a mighty spiritual principle identifies the mind with that principle; then all that the principle stands for in the realm of ideas is poured out upon the one who affirms (*The Twelve Powers of Man*, 38).

In the meditation sections in the following pages, you will find affirmations applicable to each of our twelve spiritual abilities. Affirmations are also addressed in *How to Pray Without Talking to God*, chapter 4. Here are some examples. Implant these truths in your awareness when you are most receptive, such as during prayer, after meditation, or upon awakening in the morning:

> I am naturally joyous, for my true nature is
>   divine joy.
> I am naturally loving, for my true nature is
>   divine love.
> I am naturally generous, for my true nature is
>   divine abundance.
> I tell myself the great truth: I am divine.
> God is love. I AM divine love, loving.
> God is faith. I AM divine faith, faithful.
> God is release. I AM divine release, releasing.
> God is will. I AM divine will, willing.

As you read about each of the twelve spiritual abilities in the following pages, may you discover the light of these powers within you, for they are varying views of your one true Divine Identity.

Physical centers of light corresponding to the twelve powers

1

THE LIGHT OF FAITH— THE POWER OF PERCEPTION, CONVICTION, AND EXPECTANCY

Now faith is the assurance of things hoped for, the conviction of things not seen. —Hebrews 11:1

Faith is the perceiving power of the mind linked with a power to shape substance. It is spiritual assurance, the power to do the seemingly impossible. It is a force that draws to us our heart's desire right out of the invisible spiritual substance. It is a deeper inner knowing that that which is sought is already ours for the taking, the "assurance of things hoped for."

—Charles Fillmore, *Keep a True Lent*

FAITH IS THE POWER TO make the possible real. Our very sense of reality depends on faith. It is the power that realizes (that is, makes real) images held in the mind.

We all live by faith. One summer day, while floating in my backyard pool and enjoying the multilayered cloud movement overhead, I began thinking about the curvature of the Earth. The Earth is a massive sphere, I thought, which means someone and her house around the world from me should be upside down. But no one lives upside down. By means of invisible gravity, all physical matter lies on or near the surface of this enormous orb. Who in this world rises in the morning wondering whether his feet will stay on the ground rather than float up like a helium-filled balloon? Who questions whether the sun will rise or the sidewalk will hold? Who worries that the backyard fig tree might produce pomegranates this season? We live by faith, perceiving a reality that cannot be seen with human eyes; convinced that invisible principles have real effects; and expecting life to unfold accordingly.

To externalize faith is to disclaim our spiritual power. Faith's power is not in someone or something *else*. Faith is not the same as *belief in*. Those who say they have faith in another person or in God believe that someone outside themselves has the power to control, to fix, and to eliminate human problems. Yes, belief in God, as in "God will come through for us; He just *has* to," presumes a personality God that is a superhuman superhero. GOD is not a someone who *acts* but a principle that *is*.

Faith is our innate power to create our reality by our perceptions, our beliefs, and our interpretations. According to our faith, we live in assurance/conviction. According to our faith, we expect.

Perception

Our faith is based upon our perception, which is our awareness or consciousness. We experience a reality formed when we interpret our observations about life, our impressions about the world's state of affairs, and our beliefs accumulated through the years. Many years ago I had a conversation with a neighbor who felt certain God was soon to destroy Earth and save the chosen few. Based upon her learned interpretation of Christian scriptures, my neighbor claimed the time was ripe for God's final judgment. She pointed to a rising crime rate, diminishment of family values, and various local social problems as evidence of a degenerate humanity. Changing patterns in nature, such as recent volatile weather, bolstered her premise that the world and most of its people were unworthy of salvation. I remember walking back to my house feeling stunned, shaking my head in amazement. Never, not once, had I perceived the world the way my neighbor had. Instead, my perception was of an increasingly conscientious world where people were thinking globally and acting locally to feed hungry children and house the homeless. Where my neighbor perceived a world perverted by godlessness, I perceived a rising consciousness of goodness.

After Dr. Martin Luther King Jr.'s "I Have a Dream" speech in August 1963, NBC aired a prime-time documentary anchored by the network's Chet Huntley. Huntley said about his childhood in Montana: "We never really looked with honesty at Negroes the way we examined the anatomy of a grasshopper, say, or speculated on the after-hours life of a teacher. We looked, but we had been told what to see" (Branch, "Remembering the March").

Our perception is so critical to our experience of reality that it would be wise for us to question our perception and to seek the greatest truth we can fathom as the basis for our viewpoint. Truth is spiritual law, or principle, about the immutable and benevolent nature of GOD. Truth is about our innate spiritual capacities—love, life, faith, judgment, etc. Truth is the interconnectedness of all life and the order existing within all of creation. Truth is the principle of giving and receiving not as reciprocity but as a simultaneous activity. Truth is the law of compensation that proves the adage, "When one door closes, another opens." Truth is the eternality of life and the essential GODness/goodness of all people.

Two particular perceptions support powerful faith: our perception of the absolute truth, or spiritual principle, underlying all human/material conditions, and our perception of possibilities.

In order to perceive the absolute truth that is ever-present and independent of material conditions, we must rely on ESP. Yes, extrasensory perception! Everyone is capable of disregarding *what is* long enough to sense—to be sensitive to—what is really going on, spiritually, behind the veil of materiality.

No one has more need for faith than when experiencing distressing human conditions such as illness, loneliness, poverty, or conflict. When wracked by pain from an injury, for example, it is challenging to perceive the absolute wholeness of life. However, relying upon the principle of life—animation, vitality, and presence—is precisely the key to relief and healing. Perceiving the animating principle at work in every cell of the body, becoming aware of a limitless source of energy within and around us, and seeing that a temporary condition cannot diminish our wholeness of being are generative and restorative thoughts. Adhering to these principles anchors us to a faith that perceives what cannot be sensed by only-human faculties, as Winifred Wilkinson Hausmann tells us:

> Faith is that quality in us which enables us to look past appearances of lack, limitation or difficulty, to take hold of the divine idea and believe in it even though we do not see any evidence of it except in our mind. Through faith we know with an inner knowing the Truth that has not yet expressed in our manifest world (Hausmann, *Your God-Given Potential*, 38).

Our power to perceive extends to future possibilities. Our perception of possibilities is influenced by all we have concluded about life. Pessimism and hopelessness pervading dinner table-talk during our childhood may haunt us in adulthood, for example. Fortunately, we are never forever beholden to our past. Our ability to perceive ever more desirable possibilities is innate and can be exercised.

Possibilities exist in the invisible realm, the yet-unformed state of mind. Jesus of Nazareth's kingdom of God, aka the kingdom of the heavens, is the realm of infinite possibilities. The invisible realm contains the ideal—perfect life, unconditional love, unfailing wisdom, overflowing abundance, perpetual expansion, continuous creativity, and all possibilities that ever were or ever could be. Jesus said this kingdom, or state of mind, "is spread out upon the earth, and people don't see it" (Thomas 113b). Also, "the kingdom of God is not coming with things that can be observed; nor will they say, 'Look, here it is!' or 'There it is!' For, in fact, the kingdom of God is among you" (Luke 20b–21).

The wielder of the greatest power of faith is one who not only perceives possibilities but who views the *impossible* as possible. "Ordinary people believe only in the possible. Extraordinary people visualize not what is possible or probable, but rather what is impossible. And by visualizing the impossible, they begin to see it as possible" (Cherie Carter-Scott, www.goodreads.com). A favorite poem my daughter Alicia and I read together when she was little comes from celebrated children's author Shel Silverstein. "Listen to the Mustn'ts" advised children that the impossible isn't: "Anything can happen, child. ANYTHING can be" (Silverstein, *Where the Sidewalk Ends*, 27).

Exercising faith by perceiving the truth hidden within the facts and seeing great possibilities in impossible situations leads to another aspect of faith: conviction.

Conviction

One Christmas, when my son Adrian was three and a half years old, Santa Claus visited our home. Adrian had already gone to bed. I woke him as our neighbor in a Santa Claus costume was entering our front door, just below Adrian's bedroom. Santa's bells were jingling. When I told Adrian Santa was on his way up the steps to visit him, Adrian's eyes widened in wonder. He felt sure he had heard Santa and his reindeer on the roof. He heard the jingle bells as Santa arrived at his bedroom door. Adrian was transfixed during his brief visitation, after which he swiftly fell back to sleep. For years afterward, Adrian could not be dissuaded about the reality of Santa Claus, no matter how insistent his friends and even his younger sister were. It wasn't so much the costumed man who had stood in his bedroom that night—he saw many other Santa representatives over the years at the mall and in storefronts. It was what Adrian had *not* seen, but sensed, that convinced him. He had heard reindeer's hooves on the roof and Santa's bells ringing, and he had felt Christmas enchantment.

Conviction is the mindset of faith. Conviction is trust, assurance, confidence. In trust, we do not need to perpetually recite affirmations or keep a desire afloat like juggling pins that need our constant attention to stay above the ground. The fruit of trust is a peaceful mind.

A farmer interviewed a potential farmhand whose only self-stated success had been "I can sleep through a storm." Needing help right away and taking a liking to him, the farmer hired the man. Soon after, a wicked storm struck during the night. The farmer called for his farmhand who did not hear him because he was fast asleep. On his own, then, the farmer walked outdoors and found the farmhouse shuttered, the barn shut tight, bales of hay protected by tarps, the tractor secured in the garage, animals enclosed with supplies of food and water—everything in its place. In a flash of awareness, the farmer understood why his employee could sleep through a storm. He faithfully did his work, preparing for all conditions, and therefore could sleep peacefully every night.

Living in conviction is living from a prepared consciousness, in trust of the truths and possibilities that exist under the surface of material existence. Living in trust is living the way I would live in fulfillment of my heart's desire. When experiencing physical symptoms of disease, I exercise faith in my essential wholeness, living as a whole person lives—I do what I can every day in support of my health, vitality, and well-being.

In early 1979, when I announced my engagement to Giles, of African descent, my Italian father renounced me. During the nine years my father was absent from my life, I kept my heart and mind open to him, convinced of the possibility within the seeming impossible. Impossible because of many repeated experiences of my father's rejection: He would hang up the telephone when he heard my voice on the line, he refused to attend my brothers' weddings if I would be invited, and he walked out the back door of the funeral parlor during my maternal grandmother's viewing when I walked in the front door. It would have been easy for me to harbor bitterness and hatred, but I chose instead to live convinced that love, our true nature, would triumph. Although plenty of discouraging thoughts and feelings crept in along the way, I faithfully held to the promise of love—the magnetizing, harmonizing, and unifying power. When I thought of Dad, I envisioned our reunion embrace rather than fixate on his rejection of my family and me. I gave my children an image of their grandfather as someone who would love them if he knew them, someone who was struggling to understand that a different skin color does not make a person different from him. I planted within my children's hearts a sense of hope for one day knowing their grand-pop. I maintained that sense of hope myself as well.

> Faith is the highest expression of belief or confidence. It is that something in man which says: "I believe in the possibilities of things that I cannot see. I believe in the possibility of Divine Mind doing in this age, right now, everything that was ever done in any age." When we believe this and hold to it, putting aside all doubt and whatever

suggests failure, the thoughts of faith begin to accumulate substance, and fulfillment follows (Fillmore, *Atom-Smashing Power of Mind*, 74).

Living in conviction, we maintain a sense of positive expectancy.

Expectancy

Expectancy is another aspect of faith. Faith is demonstrated by a general sense of joyous anticipation. I expect things to go well. I expect to know how to respond moment by moment. I expect to act intentionally. I expect to feel blessed. I expect meaningful, rich experiences. I know universal GODness/goodness. I see possibilities, especially in impossible situations. I live convinced of my spiritual capacities to unify, balance, discern, create, realize, uphold, etc. Living in a state of positive expectancy, I become a powerful positive force in the world.

Charles Fillmore described potent physical and spiritual effects of expectancy this way:

> Faith is of the mind and it is the match that starts the fire in the electrons and protons of innate spirit forces . . . When the trillions of cells in one's body are roused to expectancy by spiritual faith, a positive spiritual contact results and marvelous transformations take place (Fillmore, *Atom-Smashing Power of Mind*, 14).

A farming community suffered during a protracted drought. The parched earth produced little of the life- and wealth-sustaining crop every family depended upon. A local minister called the community together to pray for rain. The town square became crowded with citizens from all faith traditions. The minister greeted everyone, scanning the crowd for familiar faces. The minister's eyes landed on a young girl approaching from the rear. The crowd parted as she neared. She was carrying her umbrella.

Convinced that divine love united my father and me eternally, I reminded myself for nearly nine years that nothing could separate us. I believed that if he—or I—were to die before we reconciled, our physical separation could not possibly interfere with our bond of love. I believed this because despite my suffering from his renunciation, I also cared about his well-being and knew in my heart that he cared about mine. Human emotions aside, we were bound together by divine love, the unifying power.

On Thanksgiving Day in 1987, almost nine years after he had disowned me, my father reclaimed me. I do not take credit for the miracle of reconciliation between Dad and me, but I credit faith—my power of perception, conviction, and expectancy. Faith moved that mountain.

Meditation for Faith

Calming my breath, I focus attention on the center of my forehead inward, at the site of the pineal gland located between the two hemispheres of my brain. Breathing in and breathing out, attention fixed, I bless this connecting link between the physical and the spiritual. Sensitive to the pulsing of life, the movement of energy, I shine the royal blue light of faith into the center of my brain. The spaces between the hemispheres brushed blue, I broadcast blue light throughout my brain and down through my body—a healing, streaming royal blue signifying my consciousness of faith.

Faith is my ability to see what cannot be seen humanly. I activate this spiritual power, courageously perceiving a greater truth than my physical senses report. I dare myself to see what cannot be seen by human eyes but exists as surely as the sun exists behind a cloud. I perceive the bottom-line truths about life: that life is irrepressible, eternal, and perfect in every stage and form. I stretch my capacity to see the good that can be in troubling situations. I envision possibilities even in seemingly impossible circumstances. I am devoted to perceiving the good that can be.

I am convinced that the nature of unseen good, the animating and harmonizing creative power behind all that I have and experience, is my nature—I am divine. I reach inward to my storehouse of faith to remain faithful during times when my human brain cannot envision the magnificent possibilities of wholeness of life, harmonious love, and wealth beyond measure. I demonstrate conviction by living as love lives, as wholeness lives, as wisdom lives. I audaciously trust in universal goodness, so much so that I rest deeply in the peace of spiritual assurance.

By my innate power of faith, I live in positive expectancy. I center my attention in joyous anticipation, knowing all is well, truly.

Practices to Cultivate Faith

1. Read the Meditation for Faith daily, or make an audio recording and listen to it daily. Choose one of the affirmations in the meditation to recite and contemplate.

2. Write about faith in your journal. Here are some questions you might choose to reflect upon:

- When have I dared to suspend my judgment about a person or situation to perceive a deeper truth?

- Thinking about the future, what have I been dreaming about doing, or being, or having? Without censoring or tempering, what are the most outrageously wonderful possibilities?

- In what seemingly hopeless situations have I held to hope, even when friends advised against it? What actions did I take that demonstrated my conviction?

- What does faithfulness mean to me? What does faithfulness look like in practice?

3 Create or select a symbol for faith and display it where you will see it often. Here are some examples: a royal blue-colored bead; a mustard seed; a photograph of the night sky; an original drawing or sculpture.

4. When walking, dancing, swimming, or participating in any form of aerobic exercise, repeat the following in rhythm with your movements:

I live in faith,
perceive the good,
trust all is well,
and expect the best.

2

THE LIGHT OF UNDERSTANDING— THE POWER OF COMPREHENSION, REALIZATION, AND INSIGHT

If you indeed cry out for insight, and raise your voice for understanding; if you seek it like silver, and search for it as for hidden treasures—then you will understand {have reverence for} the Lord and find the knowledge of God.

—Proverbs 2:3–5

Spiritual understanding is the ability of the mind to apprehend and realize the laws of thought and the relation of ideas one to another.

—Charles Fillmore, The *Revealing Word*

THE BIBLICAL PROPHET DANIEL, OF the lion's den fame, interpreted dreams for the non-Jewish kings controlling Babylon between 600 and 535 BCE. Writings about Daniel portray a dreamer and visionary, a man who regularly engaged in spiritual practices such as prayer, fasting, and acts of repentance. On one occasion while he was praying, "the man Gabriel, whom I had seen before in a vision, came to me in swift flight at the time of the evening sacrifice. He came and said to me, 'Daniel, I have now come out to give you wisdom and understanding'" (Daniel 9:21-22).

Wisdom and understanding are two distinct spiritual abilities. Wisdom arises in the moment, as needed. Wisdom is our innate ability to know the way to go, based on spiritual judgment, discernment, and intuition. Wisdom is in the gut, centered in the second brain, aka solar plexus.

Spiritual understanding is comprehending, internalizing, and then living the truth we know. Understanding dawns over time and through study and reflection, or it can come in a flash—suddenly the light shines. The seat of understanding in the physical body is the brain's frontal lobe. The intellect is engaged in understanding, but intellect alone does not produce spiritual understanding.

If knowledge is acquiring facts, understanding is making sense of those facts and forming connections between them. Understanding ultimately goes beyond fleeting facts to settle on changeless truths. Preceding understanding is a *desire* to understand:

> Ask, and it will be given you; search, and you will find; knock, and the door will be opened for you. For everyone who asks receives, and everyone who searches finds, and for everyone who knocks, the door will be opened (Matthew 7:7–8).

Desire may be conscious or not, direct or not. Daniel prayed and fasted in his desire for understanding. Curiosity is desire. Worry is desire. Confusion is desire. Doubt is desire. Desire summons understanding. Fillmore taught, "No one ever attained spiritual consciousness without striving for it" (*The Twelve Powers of Man*, 44).

Jesus' disciple Thomas, known as *doubting* Thomas, represents the power of understanding. Thomas, who loved Jesus and was in mourning after Jesus' crucifixion, doubted his friends' reports that Jesus had overcome death. Thomas told his friends, "Unless I see the mark of the nails in his hands, and put my finger in the mark of the nails and my hand in his side, I will not believe" (John 20:25b). Later Jesus appeared in a vision wherein Thomas became convinced that his teacher was indeed alive.

Thomas stands for our doubts about the invisible truths in life. Jesus represents our Divine Identity, that aspect of our nature that consists of all divine capacities—our GODness/goodness. Our Jesus or Christ nature is eternal and independent of physicality. Our inner doubting Thomas seeks to understand our eternal divine nature.

Understanding is the power of comprehension, realization, and insight.

Comprehension

Comprehension is our ability to discover connections between thought and feeling, between the body's messages and our habits of thought, between accumulated beliefs and unadulterated truth. Through comprehension we make sense of seemingly incompatible or unrelated ideas. We learn about aspects of our own Divine Identity when listening to our life.

One day in December 1989, I handed my boss a letter of resignation. Conditions had become intolerable at my workplace, an insurance company where I managed a nationwide car rental insurance program. An underwriter who had joined my department weeks before was acting in bizarre, inappropriate ways. I would overhear her in the next cubicle violently cursing at our insureds over the telephone; she would berate my staff publicly, and snicker at me menacingly whenever she would pass me in the hall. She told an employee that she carried a pistol in her purse, emphasizing that everyone had better leave her alone, or else. Members of my staff were terrified of this woman, so much that many of them left the building at the end of each day with a buddy. I had been feeling unfulfilled in my work, and this unpleasant turn of events clinched my resolve. I decided that it was time for me to resign, so I gave two weeks, notice.

The next morning, the underwriter verbally accosted another of my employees, who came to me in tears. I finally informed my boss, the vice president of the claims department. By the end of that day, the underwriter was escorted out of the building. She had been fired.

My boss asked me if my resignation had anything to do with the recent trouble, and would I reconsider staying. I said I would have an answer the next morning.

Fact is, I had been thinking about resigning from my job for quite a while. I wanted to write a book about the triumphant healing between my father and me which had begun in 1987. I wanted to be at home when my children arrived home from school, as they were growing too old for after-school day care. My husband Giles and I had talked about it for many months, imagining how we could manage financially without my salary.

That evening, I reflected back to earlier job resignations. Every time I had left a job, it had been because of something I declared intolerable. I had waited for something to go wrong before giving notice in past jobs. As I looked at my life, I could see a pattern of staying too long, staying beyond the point of satisfaction, or staying because I had not had the courage to leave without provocation. Even when I had a positive reason for leaving, a next purpose to fulfill, I would not permit myself to release the job until conditions became unbearable.

Bolstered by a fresh awareness, I realized that I was eager to let go of this job, not because anything was wrong with my work or the company but because I had a next purpose to achieve. Giles and I affirmed that we would do whatever was necessary for me to have a year off to write and be at home. I left that job honoring the work, my colleagues, and myself. I affirmed my essential worth and my capacities for order, wisdom, and understanding.

Comprehension comes from listening to your life. A life review, a hallmark of recovery programs and other personal development systems, shines a spotlight on our long-held beliefs, patterns of thought, and habits of behavior. Activating our innate power of understanding, we see the past in a context of wholeness. We discover the spirit of our own being, what we know of our self. We engage with our deepest longings and sense of purpose.

Charles Fillmore taught, "There are two ways of getting understanding. One is by following the guidance of Spirit that dwells within, and the other is to go blindly ahead and learn by hard experience" (*The Revealing Word*, 204).

Taking the time to reflect and listen to my life, I was able to comprehend aspects of my Divine Identity. Learning, studying, reflecting, and meditating all reward us with a growing sense of spiritual comprehension. These practices result in our claiming of our "Daniel" nature assured that "I have now come out to give you wisdom and understanding" (Daniel 9:22).

Realization

Realization is either a flash of understanding or a gradual dawning of awareness. Realization comes as a result of growing comprehension; where comprehension can be effortful, realization is effortless: "It came to me!" "Suddenly I knew what it all meant!" "It was revealed to me!"

A full 40 percent of Bible stories are written in the form of visions or dreams. An effective method for teaching spiritual principles, storytelling through visions or dreams appeals not only to the intellect but also to the heart. Take, for example, this story about the patriarch Jacob: "Jacob was left alone; and a man wrestled with him until daybreak" (Genesis 32:24). This, the first line of a short story, reveals that Jacob was dreaming. Otherwise, how could Jacob be both alone and in the company of another person?

Jacob was disturbed when he went off by himself on the night of this story. His history was catching up with him. He had betrayed his brother Esau many years prior, stealing his inheritance by trickery. He then had fled his brother's fury, settling with extended family and working in his maternal uncle's livestock business. He had married his beloved cousin Rachel, but only after Rachel's father tricked Jacob into marrying her eldest sister Leah. For many years, Jacob had prospered in business and family life. Now, however, he learned that his brother Esau was searching for him with an army of men. Jacob had issues! He felt fearful. He felt guilty. He felt remorseful. In this state of mind, Jacob wrestled with his own spirit, his true Self. The finite self grappled with the Infinite Self, seeking understanding. Jacob insisted, "I won't let you go until you bless me" (Genesis 32:26).

Jacob awoke from his dream with an understanding of his responsibility to his family and ready to shine the light of his true nature after years of hiding.

Early one Saturday morning, I awoke from a dream I recalled in detail. I was in a luxurious, enormous spa containing a bathtub the size of a large room. Bright blue water was flowing over the top of the pool and spilling onto the floor. Concerned about flooding, I wanted to turn off the spigot, but the only way to get to the spigot was through the water. I ran, so to speak—I experienced it in slow motion—and found after turning off the spigot that water was still running. There was another spigot. And a third spigot.

Lying still in bed that early morning, I sensed importance in the images of my dream. At the time, I was feeling overwhelmed with work and neglecting physical and spiritual practices. I knew that water represents baptism, or cleansing of emotion. The three spigots spoke to me of body, mind, and spirit—my need and desire to harmonize my life and experience wholeness of being. In the dream I was in a spa, an environment in which to relax and rejuvenate. I understood that I had been longing to reconnect with all of my magnificent self and that by slowing down I could relish the gifts of my body, mind, and spirit.

How often have you awakened in the middle of the night with a flash of knowledge, a clear revelation, an answer to a pressing question? How many times have you read a billboard's message and found the hair on your arms raising in ratification of your sense of direction? A mystical divine visitation, a sensed voice of God, a sudden absolute knowing all relate to realization—our innate capacity to understand. Whereas comprehension engages our intellect, realization arises from our heart, which Charles Fillmore considered another brain—the center of the spirit of truth:

> In its beginnings this seemingly strange source of knowledge is often turned aside as a daydream; again it seems a distant voice, an echo of something that we have heard and forgotten. One should give attention to this unusual and usually faint whispering of Spirit in man. It is not of the intellect and it does not originate in the skull. It is the development, in man, of a greater capacity to know himself and to understand the purpose of creation . . . (*The Twelve Powers of Man*, 39).

Insight

Insight is our capacity to employ realization in particular circumstances—applied understanding. You can cultivate insight, for example, into your conflict with your boss or your child's sudden withdrawal. The more you have comprehended and realized spiritual truths, the more likely your insights will be accurate and useful.

Insight is not cold calculation, but spiritual intelligence arising in both the head and the heart, as Jacob Needleman suggests:

> The mind, the intellect is not simply the logical, analytic, or even intuitive organ located in the head. The real mind, the real instrument of under- standing, is a blending of at least two fundamental sources of perception—the intellect and the heart; the intellect and genuine feeling . . . that genuine feeling is not the same thing as emotional reaction (Needleman, *What Is GOD?*, 54).

What if, in daily life, we were accompanied by a film crew to whom we could signal at any time, "Stop! Take two!" In the grocery store parking lot one day, I observed a woman move her bags from a cart into her car and then leave the cart next to her car as she drove away. My inner girl scout started twitching. My dutiful citizen persona reared its judgmental head, and I blasted this woman, in my own mind, for her selfish and rude behavior. "Imagine if everyone left their carts anywhere they wanted in the parking lot! I'd bet you wouldn't be too happy to drive onto the lot and find no place to park for the carts left like litter in all the stalls! I'll show you what it means to be a good citizen! I'll take that cart and place it where you should have placed it, in the designated cart slot! Bah!"

Stop! Take two! Activating my innate power of under- standing, I sought to comprehend some of the benign reasons why someone would leave a grocery cart in a non-designated spot in a parking lot. I listened to my own life, remembering times when I was in an inordinate hurry perhaps with an ill child waiting at home for medicine; where a few more footfalls would seem exhausting at the end of a long day; or when I was mentally fixated on a problem such that I was in a state of non-awareness. Had I ever disregarded the rules—or had I ever *wanted* to disregard the rules?

My reverie led to a simple realization: Compassion is the fruit of understanding. I could think, feel, and act with compassion. Insight led me to kindly take that cart into the store, free from judgmentalness and blame, grateful to have a cart and blessing the woman who left it for me.

Insight is my sense of understanding, deeply, that my neighbor and I are cut from the same cloth—that we are one. Insight is my awareness of how to respond rather than react—how to behold the inherent good in others as well as myself, and then how to behave in light of the truth. Insight is not psychologizing another person. Insight is present awareness of others'—and my own—divine humanity and Divine Identity.

Asking/seeking leads to study, meditation, reflection—comprehension. Comprehension supports realization and realization thinking/acting. Comprehension and realization facilitate insight—the ability to see the truth in the midst of circumstance.

Meditation for Understanding

Centering my awareness above my brow and inward to the front of my brain, I locate the physical seat of spiritual understanding. I inhale and exhale intentionally, drawing breath into this area of my brain responsible for logic, mental association, planning, and impulse control. I shine the light of understanding, precious golden threads, throughout my frontal lobes, cleansing my brain and clearing foggy thinking and misunderstanding.

I AM the power of understanding, listening to my life and making meaningful connections between my experiences, thoughts, beliefs, and feelings. I comprehend my essential eternal nature as I pause in this moment of stillness.

I sit in silence for a little while. I call forth from within my realization ability, at ease knowing that flashes of awareness may come as I arise from the silence or as I move about my day.

I AM spiritual insight, seeing beneath the words and actions of others their true spiritual nature and my own. Compassion is the fruit of my insight. Understanding oneness, I act in ways that foster unity.

Divine understanding is my spiritual name and nature. Through my complementary powers of understanding and will, I am willing to understand. I am willing to suspend judgmentalness about others and myself, and to understand the divine intentions underneath each appearance. I AM divine understanding.

By the power of understanding, I learn from my life. By the power of understanding, I learn from the One Mind through which I realize eternal truths. I AM divine understanding.

Practices to Cultivate Understanding

1. Read the Meditation for Understanding daily, or make an audio recording and listen to it daily. Choose one of the affirmations in the meditation to recite and contemplate.

2. Write about understanding in your journal. Here are some questions you might choose to reflect upon:

- Thinking about your adolescence and recalling a particular event or period of time, what do you remember of your hopes and concerns? Your budding talents and consuming interests? How have the character traits you developed back then contributed to your life today?

- List significant dreams, visions, or flashes of realization that you remember. For each one, what was its message? What impact did it have on your life?

- Write about a time when you misunderstood another person's words or actions and later learned what he or she actually meant. What strategies have you developed, or could you employ, to avoid jumping to conclusions and instead seek understanding?

- Write about your understanding of GOD. How has your understanding changed through the years? Who and what have influenced your current understanding?

3. Create or select a symbol for understanding to display where you will see it often. Some examples: a gold star or coin; a light bulb or flashlight; an original drawing, collage, or sculpture.

4. Rest in the yoga posture Balasana, or Child's Pose, with your forehead touching the floor. Notice that the ground stands under you, providing a foundation for your body. Likewise, your Divine Identity, which is the ground of your being, provides the foundation for your spiritual understanding. Rest. Be still.

3

THE LIGHT OF WILL—THE POWER OF CHOICE, COMMITMENT, AND WILLINGNESS

You will decide on a matter, and it will be established for you, and light will shine on your ways.

—Job 22:28

The will is the executive faculty of the mind and carries out the edicts of the I AM.

—Charles Fillmore, *Christian Healing*

HAVE YOU NOTICED THAT HUMAN willpower is insufficient to carry us from an idea to its fulfillment? Personal or human will is behind our New Year's resolutions that dissipate after a few weeks or the need for course corrections after making choices we regret. Our brains favor survival and safety, which means we tend to exert our will in the direction of self-preservation.

Our human, finite self-awareness is subjective; we want what *we* want. Our desires are shortsighted; we want what we want without regard to long-range ramifications or the needs and desires of others. Even when we believe we are making choices with the good of all in mind, our brains are all about me, me, me. I am not faulting our brains; it's how they work. When we rely entirely on personal or human willpower, though, our willfulness becomes a handicap to fulfillment.

Humankind has suffered from willfulness. Willfulness is behind most of the world's big problems, from genocide to global warming. Every known religion recommends seeking a greater will or higher purposefulness. Christianity points to Jesus' teaching about prayer—"your will be done on earth as it is in heaven" (Matthew 6:10)—and his act of prayer in the Garden of Gethsemane—"not my will but yours be done" (Luke 22:42)—as models for the development of spiritual will.

These Bible verses are ripe for reinterpretation after centuries of lost culture and mistranslation. What comes to mind for most people raised in Western Christianity when reading the Matthew verse is a God-being that is in charge of everything and causes everything to happen or not happen. It must be God's will that your child was struck with paraplegia after being tackled on the football field. It must be God's will that you were promoted ahead of others in your company. It must be God's will that nearly three hundred people died during Hurricane Sandy.

The English word *will* in this verse, recognized as a line in the Lord's Prayer, has been translated from the Greek word *thelema*, which means "a determination, whether by choice or inclination." A choice can be either a purpose (intention) or a decree. Will as an inclination refers to a desire or pleasure.

Thinking of God not as a supernatural person but as the One Power or One Mind underlying and throughout all that is, what could constitute "your will on earth as it is in heaven"? What could be the universal or heavenly will? Heaven represents the unified field, the invisible space within which all things are possible. You and I enter the heavenly state when we pray, meditate, and focus one-pointedly in a moment of possibilities. When we pray, meditate, and focus upon possibilities, we are in a visionary state of being in which we align with our Divine Identity or Christ consciousness. In this awareness, our will is *the* will—the universal ideal of eternal life, infinite love, ever-present wisdom, and all that is good prevailing. Our will is for the universal ideal (in heaven) to permeate the stuff and circumstances of our human existence (on earth).

In short, by this interpretation we affirm: May I bring into the microcosm the good inherent in the macrocosm. May I envision and live out the unifying power of divine love at the heart of all that is. Nowhere in this interpretation is it presumed that a supernatural being wills or demands a particular course of action from any human. No condition or circumstance is sent to us by the will of any superior sentient being. In other words, God cannot require us to do anything, and God cannot be a doer of anything, because God is not like a person. GOD, the One Mind and Power throughout the cosmos, *is* eternal life, infinite love, ever-present wisdom, and all spiritual power. Therefore "your will" is the fulfillment of life, love, and wisdom—and all spiritual power.

Carrying this interpretation into Jesus' heart-wrenching Gethsemane realization, I believe Jesus recognized that his human will would be to save himself the trouble ahead. He held in mind, however, a higher value, a sense of purpose as a Jewish teacher with a universal message about the law of love overriding religious law. His "not my will" acknowledged his human dread of the terrible position he was in. His "but yours be done" marked his acquiescence to his overarching purpose which was more important than his human safety.

When and where have you perceived yourself to be at a crossroads between self-serving, personal desires and your grander sense of purpose? Years ago, I felt inspired to apply to Unity's ministerial school, or seminary. I believed that in ministry I would utilize all my talents and passions and support the spiritual growth of many others. At the time, my two children were in their early teens, and our family was living in Omaha, Nebraska. I had worked out in my mind, and had my husband Giles's agreement, that I would live at Unity Village, near Kansas City, Missouri, during the week and drive home on weekends. Giles would be a single parent during the week, which seemed fine since I had done so for periods of time throughout Giles's military career, from which he had retired.

I stepped through a tedious process of application and interviews, after which I learned that I had not been accepted into seminary. A few months later, one of my children revealed a need for professional therapy, which I would have missed had I lived apart from my family during that time. I could have spared myself feelings of failure and humiliation had I realized through spiritual discernment that my desire to support my family was, at the time, more important than my desire to be a minister. I realized it only in retrospect. But I did get it—"your will," the greater good, is what I most desired. Ministry was never denied me by God's will. It was only delayed by a more pressing need. A few years into the future, when our children were launched into young adulthood, the timing was perfect for fulfillment of my calling into ministry.

Spiritual will is not submitting my personal will to an invisible superhuman being; being told through any other person what I should or should not do; subjugating my conscience or consciousness to any coercive influence, including religious dogma; or imposed as a lesson or punishment. Spiritual will is our power of choice, commitment, and willingness.

Choice

The choosing power of will is our ability to desire one possibility among infinite possibilities and to select it. Desire is the driver of choice-making. We cannot have what we do not want, not because it is denied us but because it is not in our view. We cannot see, or be, or have what we do not desire.

Desire is natural to our Divine Identity. Ever-evolving divine life demands increase and expansion of consciousness. At the heart of all humanity is a divine discontent that propels us toward more conscious, intentional, spiritual living. Therefore, although it is true that we cannot see, or be, or have what we do not desire, we have no problem desiring. Desire is innate.

Desire often springs from dissatisfaction: You feel defeated after working hard to accumulate funds for a vacation only to need that money for unexpected home repairs. You struggle with pessimism about your adult child's choices, which you cannot control. You do not feel well, and the doctor's diagnosis has not helped. You feel restless and purposeless at your job. You have much to be thankful for, and yet you feel as though something is missing.

Discontent naturally gives rise to desire. Desire may be conscious or not, direct or not. Curiosity is desire. Worry is desire. Confusion is desire. Doubt is desire. Desire searches for its next pleasure, or relief, or fulfillment. Desire opens our eyes to see among the infinite possibilities that might satisfy.

In the matter of choosing, our most successful and most spiritual activation of will follows wisdom, our power of judgment, discernment, and intuition. We activate imagination, our power of conception, vision, and creation. From infinite possibilities, we choose one. One divine idea makes sense to us. We catch hold of it. We sense its potential. We say to ourselves, "Yes, I will." Our one choice sets in motion a shift in consciousness. Whereas before we were meandering in discontent, now we are beginning upon a path toward fulfillment. Fillmore taught: "The simple statement, I will to be well, gathers the forces of mind and body about the central idea of wholeness, and the will holds the center just so long as the I AM continues its affirmation" (*Christian Healing*, 145).

Commitment

Out of infinite possibilities, I have chosen one. I determine it is mine. I resolve to follow its calling. Then I commit to it. Commitment places me on a particular path. Commitment leads not to random action but deliberate, intentional action. Choosing and following this one path means I do not choose or follow another path. I do not flit from path to path.

I one-pointedly, wholeheartedly devote myself to this path. Jesus' teaching about the narrow gate applies here:

> Enter through the narrow gate; for the gate is wide and the road is easy that leads to destruction, and there are many who take it. For the gate is narrow and the road is hard that leads to life, and there are few who find it (Matthew 7:13–14).

Fundamentalist interpreters of this Bible passage suggest Jesus' message is about heaven and hell; i.e., you'll go to heaven if you follow the strict precepts of your Christian religion and you'll go to hell if you do not. Consider instead the wisdom in this passage regarding the way we are living here and now. Jesus suggests that our life energy becomes scattered when our attention is unfocused and aimless, leading to self-destructive action. The narrow gate indicates selective attention. The "hard road" admits the human challenge of remaining centered and returning to the path when we have detoured. What is the narrow gate? For Christians, the narrow gate is devotion to Jesus and his teachings. For Taoists, it is the Tao. For Unity students, it is prayer and meditation, study, and service. For yoga practitioners, it is *asana* (posture), *pranayama* (breath work), *bhakti* (devotion), and *seva* (service). For humanists, it is the path of human decency and generosity. For all of us, the path is the plan we discern as the route to fulfilling our sense of purpose.

Getting onto the path, committing, harnesses spiritual power. The spiritual forces of creation are unleashed. We free our brains from vacillating unproductively. The energy that earlier dissipated in indecision now is directed toward being on the path.

We commit to the path itself rather than to a future point of completion of the goal. Commitment erases the past and places our attention on each footfall on the path , here and now.

When she learned she was pregnant, my cigarette-smoking friend dreamt of her baby breathing easily. She resolved to free herself from her long-standing unhealthy habit and got on the path of a nonsmoker. She committed to the path. On the path, she did not think of herself as a former smoker or a smoker on hiatus. She fulfilled the scripture, "So if anyone is in Christ, there is a new creation: everything old has passed away; see, everything has become new!" (2 Corinthians 5:17). Being "in Christ" means my friend's commitment grounded her in her true nature, her Christ consciousness, or Divine Identity, in which history is irrelevant. Her Infinite Self led the way through the narrow gate and onto a path of intentionality.

No excuses! Commitment says. Not my will but yours. Not my only-human preferences but my true desire, the desire arising out of divine discontent. No one wants to live in the clutches of compulsion. Everyone wants to be free from self-destructive and life-suppressing habits. Each of us desires to say—and mean—"I will!" to a high, expansive way of living. I will to be well. I will love unconditionally. I will appreciate life. I will respect and honor myself.

"I will" is not a promise for the future but a self-command for now. "I will" is like Genesis's "let there be." "Let me be . . ." is a command of the Infinite Self.

Commitment is the sustaining power of will. Commitment is my integrity meter. When I begin to wander away from my path, commitment pulls me back. When I have resolved to practice daily meditation, and I fall into bed after a long day during which I skipped my practice, commitment has me recognize I have not done what I said I would do. Commitment has me get up out of the bed to fulfill my promise.

No matter what, commitment says, "I am willing." When I just don't feel like it, I do it anyway. When my routine gets interrupted, when the kids make the house too chaotic over summer break, when my lover leaves or my dog dies, commitment whispers, "nevertheless, I will."

I will live in appreciation. I will devote one hour of every day to spiritual practice. I will dance daily. I will be an attentive and loving parent. I will play outdoors every week. I will affirm my Divine Identity upon waking each morning. I will listen and respond to my body's needs. I will be a blessing to others. I will be the light of the world. I am willing. I am committed. I promise.

Willingness

If commitment is the sustaining power of will, willingness is the fuel that makes commitment possible. A willing spirit is the epitome of spiritual willpower. Willingness is the antidote for willfulness.

Exercise of the will is necessary for navigating planet Earth. In material matters, willfulness equates to mental determination—an essential quality for achieving a goal and accomplishing a project. However, when wielded in a vacuum or for mere personal gain, willfulness becomes a negative attribute, the opposite of allowing. To the degree that I proceed by willfulness—I know what I want and I know how to get it—I become uncooperative with fresh divine ideas that are always flowing, and ungovernable by inner wisdom.

Fillmore cautioned: "Stubborn, willful, resistant states of mind congest the life flow" (*The Twelve Powers of Man*, 48). Left uncorrected, persistent unwillingness impedes the body's digestion, elimination, and circulation, contributing factors in disease.

Early in 1979, during my third year in residence at Kripalu Yoga Center near Reading, Pennsylvania, I was deeply rooted in my intention to live a spiritually focused life. I was devoted to learning, teaching, and serving on the path of Kripalu. I could imagine no other place or way to live. My college sweetheart, Giles, from whom I had been separated for three years, reappeared. We decided to marry. Giles was leaving for Honolulu, Hawaii, where he would be serving in the United States Air Force on a three-year tour of duty. I believed I would live all my adult life at the ashram, so I proposed we remain engaged during Giles's tour in Honolulu after which he would move to the ashram where we would marry. Giles was agreeable. He left for Honolulu and I returned to Kripalu, but on my way I reconsidered. Obstinately, I had attempted to preserve life as I had experienced it at Kripalu while asking Giles to make it his experience as well.

By the power of willingness, I stopped trying to orchestrate our future. I tapped into the spiritual power of understanding to recognize that what I most wanted was not to live forever at Kripalu, but to live a spiritually focused life. I tapped into the spiritual power of wisdom to discern that I could forge such a life with Giles no matter where we chose to reside. Willingness opened me to possibilities that I could not conceive of in a state of willfulness.

Willingness is a state of allowing. Allowing is our capacity to welcome our experience and receive its gifts. Allowing is our ability to cooperate with rather than control the flow of divine ideas.

Robert had resided in a one-room apartment for many years, in an aging building that had once been a single home. Although the property was in need of repairs, Robert dwelt there uncomplaining. Concerned lest his landlord might increase his rent, Robert never reported the broken air conditioner/heater in his room. Instead, he bundled up in winter and sweated through unbearable summer heat. He slept upon cushions on the floor to save precious space in the tiny room. He used his bathtub as a closet, bathing at the sink. Whenever friends encouraged Robert to address his apartment's problems or relocate, Robert resisted. He resolutely clung to his living arrangements, having long memories of the time his mother was alive and they shared an apartment in the same building. Also, Robert worried about being able to afford another apartment once his part-time job ended and his income consisted entirely upon social security payments.

The day came when Robert's unwillingness to improve his living situation shifted. Conditions in his rented space became unlivable when the city turned off the water. At first, Robert presumed a plumbing problem would be repaired, but then he learned that his landlord had not paid the water bill for many months. A week went by, then two. After the third week, Robert conceded and became willing to entertain a move. Within a few hours of apartment searching, Robert found a lovely one-bedroom apartment in a complex that was rent-subsidized. He would be able to stay there and contain his costs into the future. Robert put in his notice at his old apartment and signed a lease on his new place. He pinches himself in disbelief every day that he now lives in a well-kept community where he has a functional bedroom, bathroom, kitchen, and living room.

Robert's inner journey from willfulness to allowing was not easy for him. It came slowly and after significant discomfort. Eventually, though, Robert welcomed his experience. I observed delightedly how he went from trepidation to hope and from disbelief to amazement. When finally Robert chose to cooperate with rather than resist the flow of divine ideas, his face lit up with joyful expectation. His inner being felt at home the moment he stepped into the apartment that he would claim by spiritual will.

Sometimes, the change prompted by willingness is not external but internal. Sometimes, our faculty of inner wisdom indicates staying rather than leaving. In this case, willingness is accepting things as they are and finding our opportunity in the middle of our present circumstances. During a time of restlessness a few years back, I wanted to leave my job, my marriage, my house, and my profession. Having gained by years of spiritual practice, I knew I was going through a period of resistance and unwillingness. I called upon my power of will. I chose to stay until I felt certain of how to proceed. I committed to deepening practices of meditation, journaling, and expressing appreciation daily. I affirmed, over and over again, willingness to be blessed by and be a blessing in the midst of my difficult experience. Looking back now, I feel thankful that I navigated a dark time by means of the light of allowing. Today's experience of fulfillment in my ministry and my marriage ratifies my sense back then that it was not time for me to pull up stakes and depart. I am aware, too, that had I truly felt guided to leave my ministry or my marriage, or both, it would have become clear to the degree I exercised allowing. Allowing is the state of remaining flexible and alert to inner wisdom. Allowing is the state of agreement. One of my favorite passages in the Bible is this one from Job 22:24: "Agree with God, and be at peace; in this way good will come to you." Allow life to unfold, acquiesce to the truth, and cooperate with the impulse of your Divine Identity. Be centered, unruffled as time passes and light shines on your path ahead. This is the way of will.

Meditation for Will

In the brain's frontal lobe lies the energy vortex for the power of spiritual will. I concentrate my attention on this area responsible for executive functioning, such as my ability to focus verbally and visually, to remember and make connections between ideas, and to choose. I shine the silver light of will throughout the front of my brain, across my forehead, and up to the crown of my head. I clear my busy brain of preconceived notions and all false imaginings.

Centered in spiritual will, I affirm my capacity to choose. Guided by my companion powers of understanding, wisdom, and imagination, I am able to draw from infinite possibilities one divine idea. This one divine idea seems to catch hold of me. It appears as my powerful desire. It becomes rooted in my awareness as mine.

I affirm my capacity to commit to a path ahead. I will be a blessing. I will live as the light of the world. I will . . . (insert your specific commitment). I set upon a course of action that supports my choice. I live in integrity, honoring my commitment and holding myself accountable to do what I say I will do.

I affirm my willingness. I am willing. I am willing to remain attuned to the source of all good. I allow life to unfold. I acquiesce to the truth, and I cooperate with the impulse of my Divine Identity. I am willing to be centered, unruffled as time passes and light shines on my path ahead.

I am willing to courageously decide what I will have, do, and be.

I am willing to boldly reach for my next goal.

I am willing to stretch beyond perceived limits.

I am willing to walk with confidence into my future.

I am willing to risk being vulnerable in love.

I am willing to listen without feeling threatened.

I am willing to experience the joy of living today.

I am willing to be purposeful, to know I am divine.

Divine will is my spiritual name and nature.

I am willing to be the light of the world, wherever I am and whatever the circumstances.

Practices to Cultivate Will

1. Read the Meditation for Will daily, or make an audio recording and listen to it daily. Choose one of the affirmations in the meditation to recite and contemplate.

2. Write about will in your journal. Here are some questions you might choose to reflect upon:

   • In light of what you have read about the power of will and your evolution of understanding, how would you explain "GOD's will"?

- In what ways are personal will and universal will distinct?

- Remember a time when "divine discontent" led to your choosing a new direction or a productive change in life. Reflecting back, what were some of your early signs that new desires were arising? When you actually chose and then committed to a path, what was it like for you to assert the light of will?

- Describe your experience of shifting from willfulness to willingness.

3. Create or select a symbol for will to display where you will see it often. Here are some examples: a silver disc or pendant; an original drawing, collage, or sculpture.

4. Choose a sport or physical activity you have not practiced but that you believe would be beneficial and desirable. Commit yourself to a short-term period of instruction or practice, exercising the three aspects of the light of will: choice, commitment, and willingness.

4

THE LIGHT OF IMAGINATION—THE POWER OF CONCEPTION, VISION, AND EMBODIMENT

Finally, beloved, whatever is true, whatever is honorable, whatever is just, whatever is pure, whatever is pleasing, whatever is commendable, if there is any excellence and if there is anything worthy of praise, think about these things.

—Philippians 4:8

Imagination is the act or power of forming a mental image of something not present to the senses or never before wholly perceived in reality . . . a power that frees us from the limitations of our senses . . . the power of conception.

—James Dillet Freeman, *Imagination*

IMAGINATION IS OUR POWERFUL CAPACITY to picture what can be and, by holding that idea and developing it until we feel its effects while it is yet unmanifest, to live into that idea until it essentially becomes our reality. In a sense, imagination is our primary power because it is essential for the cultivation of all our magnificent spiritual capacities.

Imagination is natural to us. By age two, children are able to imagine objects that are not materially present. Imaginative play becomes a primary way children learn about life and process complicated emotions. Imagination is values-neutral, which means it is as possible for us to imagine the worst as it is for us to imagine the best.

My daughter Alicia was three years old when our family went to see the film *ET* at our local movie theater. Alicia sat on my lap through the film, still and silent. During the last scene, when Elliott tearfully says good-bye to his extraterrestrial friend, my daughter began to sob. She cried and cried until everyone had left the theater. Giles and I believed Alicia had fallen in love with ET just as Elliott had, so we purchased a large poster of ET on our way out of the theater and hung it in Alicia's bedroom. Soon afterward, Alicia began having nightmares about spiders and whales. She would fly into our bedroom during the night, heart pounding as she leapt into our bed to feel safe. Several weeks went by this way until one night Giles took Alicia back to her room and attempted to soothe her. Frozen in his arms, she was staring straight ahead, her eyes big as saucers, when Giles realized what she was afraid of. It was ET! Giles removed the poster and we all enjoyed restful sleep from that night on.

We'll never know what Alicia was imagining about ET, but as her language skills grew Alicia displayed an active imagination. As many children do, Alicia had imaginary friends, one she referred to as "bad sister." As easily as Alicia conjured frightening characters lurking under the bed and peering in through the windows, she also was able to sweep her room clean of fearful specters by assuming her superhero nature. Imagining herself powerful rather than powerless resolved the matter, time after time.

We use our power of imagination all the time. With imagination, we can travel around the world instantly, onto the second story of a tram looking out upon a collage of colorful market displays along the tramline on Hong Kong island. With imagination, we can unite our fractured families. We can bring peace to the Middle East. We can assert wholeness for an ill friend. We can celebrate success before we have begun. We can recreate our past. We can accomplish the impossible.

Our ability to imagine is paramount. It is of such prime importance that twentieth century metaphysical author Neville Goddard regarded Jesus Christ as the exemplification of the power of imagination. In Goddard's view, imagination is our redeeming ability. By the power of imagination, we can revise our past experience as well as create an ideal future. We can imagine ourselves into our true nature and assert our greatest spiritual capacities.

Charles Fillmore taught:

> The highest and best work of the imagination is the marvelous transformation that it works in character. Imagine that you are one with the principle of good, and you will become truly good. To imagine oneself perfect fixes the idea of perfection in the invisible mind substance, and the mind forces at once begin the work of bringing forth perfection (*Christian Healing*, 105).

Imagination is our power of conception, vision, and embodiment.

Conception

Any constructive idea that you or I could ever conceive of comes from the One Mind. The first three words in an English language Bible reveal this truth: "In the beginning." In the beginning, GOD. In the beginning, Good. GOD/Good is in the beginning—the origin of every vision, of every hope and dream. In the beginning, One Mind.

More revealing is the etymology of the Hebrew word *bere'shiyt*, translated into English as "beginning." *Bere'shiyt* is derived from its root *ro'sh*, which appears in the King James Version of the Bible 598 times. Fourteen times, *ro'sh* is translated as "beginning." More than 400 times, however, *ro'sh* is translated as "head," "chief," or "top." The headwaters of a river are the starting point or source, just as the source of all ideas is One Mind, out of which all ideas flow. A chief is a principal; One Mind is the principal or leading intelligence informing all ideas. The top is the summit or crown; One Mind is the highest possible source. These shades of meaning lead to the truth that all I could conceive of stems from One Mind, the origin of all that is. The beginning.

Consider the value of understanding that everything you could ever conceive of, every new and fresh idea, originates in One Mind. If you can conceive it, it already exists in One Mind! Whether it seems possible or impossible, it must be possible because it is derived from the unified field of intelligence. Do all ideas stem from One Mind, including harmful or negative ideas? We would rightfully say yes; however, harmful or negative ideas are misinterpretations or misrepresentations of One Mind intelligence. With our conceiving power, we catch an idea—which is to say we make it our own, filtering it through our human consciousness. The character of the consciousness determines the quality of its imaginings.

A fearful consciousness imagines the worst, drawing upon personal experience and a collective consciousness of fear for ideas. Many of us focusing on the worst builds up the vibration of it, actually contributing to the likelihood of the worst thing manifesting. Recessions, epidemics, and acts of mass violence are a few of the terrible consequences of fearful imaginings. A fearful consciousness can bring about actual, physical symptoms as well:

> A woman watched her little daughter pass through a heavy iron gate. The gate swung shut and the mother imagined that it had caught and crushed the little one's fingers. But the child had withdrawn her fingers before the gate struck. The mother felt pain in her own hand, and the next day she found a dark streak across her fingers, in the place where she had imagined that the child's had been crushed (Charles Fillmore, *Christian Healing*, 104).

It is helpful to know that we are equally as capable of imagining the best as the worst. In fact, imagining the best is an innate evolutionary drive that becomes easier with practice. We can practice conceiving of harmony when undergoing challenges in our relationships. We can conceive of our loved one's wholeness of being during his or her illness. We can redirect an obsessive image of an airplane crash by conceiving of the plane landing safely.

Our conceiving power is unlimited. We are constantly having bright ideas pop into our head. The more we exercise our conceiving power, and the more we allow ourselves to imagine, the more readily we recognize ideas. Desire leads to conception. You knew this, yes? It is as true mentally as it is true biologically. Our need, or desire, for solutions to problems and creative expression harness imagination. Our awareness of the conceiving power catalyzes it.

Prior to the nineteenth century, left and right shoes were identical, rather than contoured to fit each foot. So-called "straight" shoes were so uncomfortable that the idea of custom-made shoes arose. A radical and innovative idea in its day, differentiated right and left shoes are an industry standard today.

Ben Franklin grew weary of constantly putting on and taking off his two pairs of eyeglasses to adjust his near- and far-sightedness. A creative inventor, Franklin conceived of bifocals.

In the late 1800s, Thomas Adams planned to discard a stockpile of chicle, the gummy, sticky latex from the Central American sapodilla tree, after his attempts to make synthetic rubber tires out of chicle had failed. While waiting in line in a drugstore, Adams got a bright idea when a child ahead of him purchased chewing gum made of paraffin wax. The brand Chiclets was born.

Napoleon Hill's early twentieth-century adage holds true today: All achievement, all earned riches, have their beginning in an idea! (*Think and Grow Rich*, 8).

Vision

In 1984, the first cell phones sold were so limited in scope that no more than twenty-three conversations could be carried on at any time in the same service area. Nowadays, 91 percent of adults worldwide carry cell phones. Picture this: In 2004, when I visited a primitive fishing village in Hong Kong where families lived on their fishing boats, I was surprised to learn that all the children and their parents carried cell phones. At the end of their school day, children called their parents from the shore to come get them—an ingenious development born of the need for safety and efficiency.

The visioning power of imagination is our capacity to dream of what has not yet manifested, to flesh out an idea, and to feel the benefit of it in advance of its fulfillment. To envision is to create in the mind, the first and most necessary phase of creation. Studies have proven that our brains are preset to see what we are looking for, which means we continuously create more of the familiar. However, our prefrontal cortex, a recent evolutionary development, gives us the capacity to envision possibilities *beyond* our present knowledge. By this power, we can leap from what *is* to what *can be*.

Nothing has ever materialized that has not first been imagined. Our visioning capacity is the first and most important aspect of creation. Antoine de Saint Exupéry, a French writer and pioneering aviator, said: "If you want to build a ship, don't drum up the men to gather wood, divide the work, and give orders. Instead, teach them to yearn for the vast and endless sea" (Antoine de Saint Exupéry, www. imaginalinstitute.com).

In metaphysical understanding, creation occurs by the union of head and heart.

What can be, *can* be when we hold a potent idea in mind, develop it by imagining it fleshed out into manifestation, and feel the thrill of fulfillment while incubating the idea in mind.

What can be, *can* be when I hold a potent idea while I feel *now* how I expect to feel when it is fulfilled. Thinking and feeling as one creative mind activity is a preposterously simple yet underutilized practice. According to Abraham-Hicks, if we were to concentrate attention on one idea for a mere seventeen seconds, we would experience as much benefit as if we had labored full-time for an entire year.

Exercise your visioning capacity in a few moments of focus every day. If your family is fractured by disharmony among relatives, for example, your focused attention on the idea of family unity is more valuable than trying to convince each of the involved relatives to rekindle the relationship. Ask yourself, what does a harmonious family look like and feel like? Advance in your mind to a future gathering of the family. What would that gathering be like if everyone were to welcome one another in love and interact with one another respectfully? Describe your longed-for experience in the company of a harmonious family, either in writing or in spoken language. You might write or say:

> I am basking in the pure pleasure of being with my entire family gathered together. Uncle Joe and Aunt Mary are beaming with joy to be surrounded by the next three generations. Everyone has brought a contribution for the table, delectable dishes that are each person's specialty. Cousin Bob's pulled pork, sister-in-law Sue's potato salad, grandmother's butter press cookies, and my lasagna all causing mouthwatering anticipation. I wrap my arms around my cousin Joanne, whom I haven't seen in twenty years! Young nieces and nephews are

playing together, giggling, dancing, and sneaking sips of their parents' beer. I overhear brothers and sisters exclaiming, "Nothing is more important than family." I am laughing at my dad's corny jokes. I am crying with my cousin whose beloved is in declining health. My uncle is saying to his brother, "I understand." I am in love with my family.

Specifically, describe what you are doing and feeling in your vision. Every day, write your vision again, whether or not today's description is identical to yesterday's. Every time you entertain your vision, let it be as fresh as the first time and feel it as if it were your reality.

Vision is an inherent capacity, as natural as thought and feeling. So is *revision*. By our faculty of imagination, we can do what sci-fi time travelers are mandated not to do: We can revise history. We can tell ourselves a different story about our past, one that breaks the chains of habitual assumptions. For example, we can recast the fact of our adoption: Rather than having been abandoned by a birth parent, we were chosen by our adopted parent. The vibration we hold by feeling wanted energizes us and links us with positive heart's desires.

Embodiment

Imagination is perhaps the greatest tool for us to assume, and claim, our Divine Identity. The future we have been envisioning demands one thing of us: that we *be* the person who can live in that desired future. The counterpart to manifestation of an idea is embodiment, or being a living expression of the qualities required for the idea to become reality. Embodiment is the pinnacle of creation.

Who am I? And how do I live when I am on purpose, conceiving of and envisioning fulfillment? According to Neville Goddard,

> Disregard appearances, conditions, in fact all evidence
> of your senses that deny the fulfillment of your desire.
> Rest in the assumption that you are already what you
> want to be, for in that determined assumption, you
> and your Infinite Being are merged in creative unity,
> and with your Infinite Being (God), all things are pos-
> sible (*The Power of Awareness*, 63–64).

By the power of imagination, I live *as if*. I incarnate or embody the character necessary for the ideal to become real. I become the personification of fulfilled consciousness. This is what Jesus the Christ did, and it's the reason he is often named the Incarnate Word. "The word became flesh" (John 1:14) acknowledges that the word, or idea of the spiritual human, can be embodied. Jesus is revered to this day because of his comprehension of the idea of the spiritual human and his audacious embodiment of the spiritual human consciousness. Jesus accepted his Divine Identity. He understood that he was capable of spiritual power rather than limited to only-human expression. Miracles and healings associated with Jesus reveal Jesus' grasp of his spiritual capacities and his willingness to be the personification of them. The word became flesh! Picture Jesus reading the prophet Isaiah speaking as GOD:

> I am the Lord, I have called you in righteousness,
> I have taken you by the hand and kept you;

I have given you as a covenant to the people,
a light to the nations,
to open the eyes that are blind,
to bring out the prisoners from the dungeon,
from the prison those who sit in darkness.
(Isaiah 42:6–7)

Picture Jesus recognizing in these phrases a mandate for Israel (the "you" addressed in Isaiah's message was the whole of Israel) that he personalized. Israel, the nation, was made up of people. If Israel were to fulfill this mandate, it would be because people did the work. Can you sense what must have been Jesus' realization of his life's purpose? Perhaps it was to be a light to others, to open the spiritual eyes of those who are blinded by materiality, and to free those who are prisoners to their limitations.

What do you imagine is your purpose? A clue exists within your greatest desires. When you think you want a "perfect life partner who will love you unconditionally," perhaps your purpose is to be steeped in divine love, to have that love flowing in and from all directions in your life—for divine love to consume you such that you feel fulfilled in every moment. Your purpose, perhaps, is to *be* the magnetizing, harmonizing, and unifying power of love!

When you think you want "an exciting workplace where everyone works together for innovation," perhaps your purpose is to embody zeal so that you experience zeal in every circumstance. Perhaps, your purpose is to *be* zeal's capacities of enthusiasm, audacity, and devotion applied toward the improvement of conditions in the world around you.

Imagination's powers of conception, vision, and embodiment are chief among our spiritual capacities. When cultivated and activated, these abilities lead to audacious demonstrations. Like Jesus, you may begin to see yourself as a divine human here to remind others of their Divine Identity.

Meditation for Imagination

I breathe into the center of my brain, between my ears and eyes. I flood my brain with light the color of the midday cloudless sky, the palette of spiritual imagination. Every breath I take, and every breath I release, leaves me floating in the open sky of possibilities. Nothing can weigh me down. Nothing can inhibit the free expression of my divine imagination. Soaring in infinite space, all things are possible.

Divine imagination is my spiritual name and true nature. I am a creator by divine design. I reach beyond assumptions and limitations, dreaming of magnificent possibilities. By the power of conception, I catch a marvelous idea of what I can be, what I can do, and what I can experience. I can tell that this idea is mine to express by its captivating appeal. I recognize in this idea the possibility of fulfillment that I have longed for.

The marvelous idea I have grasped fleshes out as a vision and a purpose. Like a seed planted in the ground and watered, this idea is nurtured by my power of vision. I envision the fully formed blossom now, while the seed remains in the deep womb of possibilities.

I AM the spiritual power of imagination, claiming my Divine Identity. I call forth from within me my rightful divine capacities, pouring them out in fulfillment of my purpose. I have eyes to see the good within me. I have eyes to see the good around me. I have eyes to see the good path ahead of me. Whatever seems impossible, by my power of imagination I declare: All things are possible.

Practices to Cultivate Imagination

1. Read the Meditation for Imagination daily, or make an audio recording and listen to it daily. Choose one of the affirmations in the meditation to recite and contemplate.

2. Write about imagination in your journal. Here are some questions you might choose to reflect upon:

   - Listen to or read the lyrics from the late John Lennon's "Imagine." Write your own "Imagine" poem or song.

   - Rehearse your desired future by writing as if your desires are already fulfilled. What are you doing, thinking, and feeling in your fulfilled future?[4]

   - Contemplating a challenging situation in your life, answer the question, "What if it all goes well?"

   - Rewrite a painful story from your past, reinterpreting it in a way that strengthens you and lifts you up.

3. Create or select a symbol for imagination to display where you will see it often. Here are some examples: a kaleidoscope; a feather; an original drawing, collage, or sculpture.

....

[4] Note: I recommend you repeat this journal activity daily for twenty-one days to synchronize thought and feeling and increase the possibility of manifesting your desires.

4. Play like a child. Crawl on the lawn or in the woods, inspecting microscopic wildlife close to the ground; play children's music and make up your own dance; play dress-up; play hopscotch; make mud paddies.

5

THE LIGHT OF ZEAL— THE POWER OF ENTHUSIASM, AUDACITY, AND DEVOTION

Do not lag in zeal, be ardent in spirit, serve the Lord.

—Romans 12:11

Zeal—Intensity, ardor, enthusiasm; the inward fire of the soul that urges humankind onward, regardless of the intellectual mind of caution and conservatism.

—Charles Fillmore, The Revealing Word

MY CHILDHOOD FRIEND GINA MASTRANGELO had the life I wanted. Everything my family was not, Gina's was, or so it appeared in my youth. The atmosphere in my parents' home was funereal compared to Gina's. Family and friends dropped in anytime day or night at Gina's, while an unexpected visitor was rare at my house. Gina's relatives were raucous and fun; they debated world issues with gusto, competing for the floor in vocal decibels I had never heard from any of my relatives.

Her father was especially loud, often engaging in shouting debates with others and always with a twinkle in his eye. Gina enjoyed freedoms that I did not. She could yell at her parents without getting slapped for disrespect. She could play loud music in her bedroom, sleep until noon, and have friends over anytime day or night. Gina and I could sneak-smoke cigarettes in her bedroom, unlike in my house where the odor would be detected immediately. Gina, her mom, and I would linger in their kitchen after Mrs. Mastrangelo fixed us Sara Lee pound cake fried in butter, discussing many issues Gina and I were dealing with as young teens. I loved Gina's life. I frequently felt more myself in Gina's life than in my own.

But Gina's life was not what it seemed. Twenty years later, I learned that Gina's alcoholic father would scream at her mother in fits of rage, sending Gina into the closet of her attic-level bedroom to cover her ears and hide. The turbulence I had mistaken for spiritedness wore on Gina at a young age. Unbeknownst to me, her best friend through most of childhood, Gina started drinking at age fourteen.

Energy is not good or bad. Exuberance by itself is not a sign of the wielding of our power of zeal. Zeal must be tempered by understanding and wisdom. My friend Gina gained understanding about herself and her family, and she reclaimed her power of zeal, when, in her thirties, she entered a recovery program. Today, Gina is an entrepreneur passionately serving clients who have undergone mastectomies. Today, I understand my family history, and Gina's, in the light of our perpetual quest to feel alive, engaged, and enthusiastic. I too have learned to distinguish between frenetic energy and zeal. Frustrated zeal led to the extreme energies I experienced as a child: restraint in my home and rowdiness in Gina's. Frenetic energy is wasted energy, flowing out in turbulent emotions. Zeal, on the other hand, is directed energy, focusing on an ideal to be realized.

Early in my three-year residency at Kripalu in the seventies, during guru-led meditations individuals would call out, cry, arch their backs, wave their arms, and engage in all manner of "spontaneous" phenomena. Sometimes the meditation hall would appear anything but meditative. One morning, our guru interrupted meditation, crying out, "Stop!" He sensed that much of the phenomena was contrived or was not useful. He explained that phenomena are only useful if they lead to improvement in spiritual awareness. From that day forward, we were to direct the high energy of meditation inward, into silence rather than dissipating it by outwardly expressed sound and movement. Although zeal can often be observed in an effervescent personality, the potency of zeal comes from within. Zeal is an inner flame.

As is true with all of our spiritual abilities, zeal is natural to us. To eagerly awaken each day, to enthusiastically anticipate our activities, to forge ahead with gusto, to wholeheartedly attend to all that matters to us—these are common signs of our innate faculty of zeal at work. Zeal is so important that we worry when someone fails to display it, fearing clinical depression or other serious health concerns.

Spiritual zeal is the harnessing of enthusiasm as a propellant into purposeful living. Zeal is an attitude of forwardness and courageousness. Zeal is single-minded devotion to one's purpose. Zeal is our rightful power of enthusiasm, audacity, and devotion.

Enthusiasm

Zeal is enthusiasm. It is our eagerness for life, our interest in and optimism about our intentions and our plans. Zeal is noticeable. People living at high levels of zeal are often described as energetic, bright (as in filled with light), zestful, and exuberant.

I learned about the great power of enthusiasm from a master, my father.

It's Tuesday, July 28, 2009. My daughter Alicia and I spend the day with my father at Island Beach State Park in New Jersey.

Dad, at age seventy-eight, drives two and a half hours to and from the shore once or twice a week in season. He used to walk the beach and swim the ocean; nowadays his body is too frail to do all he could do in years past. He does what he can, pushing his sand cart loaded with towels, umbrella, beach chair, cooler, and all he needs for the day, pushing with one arm while leaning into his cane with the other, slowly making his half-mile pilgrimage from parking lot to seashore.

Shrunken, hardly a reflection of his younger, sturdier body, my father sets up his shrine, digging the umbrella pole a foot deep into the sand, laying out his blanket, placing his chair where sun and shade might meet. Spraying and rubbing in sunscreen, Dad uses a converted back scrubber to apply lotion where he cannot reach. After the efforts of the morning, he is tired. He prostrates before the sacred sun with a smile on his face for his first nap of the day.

The surf is rough today, so I walk alongside Dad from our spot on the beach down to the lifeguard stand where Dad deposits his cane. Quickly he assesses the situation. Sadly he realizes the undertow is too strong to hold himself upright. He explains how he often crawls on all fours into the water, his upper body still strong despite having sticks for legs. I think he is embarrassed to have his daughter see him this way. He decides not to swim out. Instead, he kneels just off the shore so that the foamy waves roll into his chest. I feel as though I am invading his privacy, a necessary spectator to his reverent ritual. The wave rushes in. He reaches out his arms, scooping the seawater up and over his hairless head, washing his face and neck and shoulders with it. Over and over again he does this, for ten minutes or more, until his knees tire.

My heart is aching for him. I want him to swim out, in a perfect crawl stroke against the current. I feel his diminished condition as a personal loss. I have no words, only my unsteady shoulder to support him and his cane back to our beach chairs. His next words surprise me. I expect he will express disappointment in his inability to ride the waves. Instead, he exclaims, "That was refreshing! There's nothing as good as the ocean."

The wind picks up around 3:00 p.m., signaling it's nearly time to pack up. Dad, trying to lower the umbrella, almost flies away on a gusty breeze. He stubbornly refuses help from Alicia and I, attempting to pack everything himself, in his order, tying all of it together in several bungee cords. Trouble is, he cannot stand against the wind for his weak lower body. Alicia spots him from behind in case the wind would unsteady him.

Sitting in backed-up traffic on the long ride home, Dad drinks his one can of warm Coke—to keep awake—and belches along with "quirky" (his word) songs from the forties on his CD player: "Mairzy Doats" (the 1943 Al Trace version) and "Open the Door, Richard!" (the 1947 Louis Jordan and his

Tympany Five version). I sit next to him in the car, making small talk, laughing over his familiar jokes, like the one when passing a cemetery: "People are dying to get in there." Seventy-eight-year-old Dad has driven five hours for one day's chance to splash in the ocean and sleep on the sand. I have to admit I am on my own pilgrimage. I ride along to witness my father's zealous adoration of earth, sky, and sea.

Nearly five years have passed since that day at the shore with my father. Dad can no longer walk unassisted. He cannot do many of the things that come easily to others, such as taking out the trash and emptying the dishwasher. Although he suffers from chronic pain, at this point he can still drive a car and he can still create one-of-a-kind stained glass masterpieces for family and friends. Friends Dad met on his favorite beach several years ago occasionally call him during the summer and arrange to meet in the parking lot near their beach. Dad drives the distance. They wait for him with a wheelchair designed to roll over sand, its wheels large and wide. Although Dad can no longer chance swimming in the ocean, his friends who are younger and stronger than him make a day at the shore possible for another avid beachgoer. When his friends celebrated their wedding anniversary last year, Dad handcrafted a beach-themed stained glass piece as his gift to them.

My father amazes me. His zest for life and his enthusiasm for each day have never diminished with age and infirmity. His way of life proves Dr. Norman Vincent Peale's message:

> Think excitement, talk excitement, act out excitement, and you are bound to become an excited person. Life will take on a new zest, deeper interest and greater meaning. You can think, talk and act

yourself into dullness or into monotony or into unhappiness. By the same process you can build up inspiration, excitement and surging depth of joy (*The Positive Principle Today*, 225).

Audacity

Audacity is an aspect of zeal relating to our inherent evolutionary impulse. Fillmore taught that zeal is the great universal force that impelling humankind to spring forward in a field of endeavor and accomplish the seemingly miraculous (*Atom-Smashing Power of Mind*, 26). Our power source for moving in the direction of fulfillment and beyond the bounds of perceived limitations is audacity, the quality of boldness and forwardness.

Audacity is a necessary quality for successful human living. Without the forward thrust of audacity, we humans would crumble under the weight of the kinds of troubles that befall all of us, such as illness, loss, and failure. In 2007, the Center for the Intrepid opened at Fort Sam Houston in San Antonio, Texas. CFI serves over 140 different wounded warriors weekly, providing "state-of-the-art amputee care, assisting patients as they return to the highest levels of physical, psychological and emotional function" (www.bamc.amedd.army.mil). Visitors to CFI are inspired by the palpable energy of the place where wounded military service personnel discover that their loss of limbs cannot impede their fulfilling futures. Intrepid, indeed!

Audacity is a strong attribute equally subject to negative or positive interpretation. A person behaving audaciously may be regarded as pushy or presumptuous, or as spunky and daring. Audacity is therefore not always regarded as a positive personality trait; however, as a spiritual power audacity is our capacity for boldly proceeding in the direction of our intentions. I believe audacity is what Marianne Williamson referred to in her often-quoted message: "Your playing small does not serve the world. There is nothing enlightened about shrinking so that other people won't feel insecure around you. We are all meant to shine" (*A Return to Love*, 191).

Audacious is the eight-year-old student in San Antonio who addressed the city council to oppose fee increases for dance classes. Audacious is the young man who celebrated his twenty-fifth birthday by raising money to purchase a school bus for students in Nepal. Audacious is the woman whose face scarred by another's brutality does not deter her from appearing in public as an advocate for women's empowerment. Audacious is the student who failed math but returns the next semester with winning strategies. Audacious is you when you courageously overcome seeming obstacles in service to a compelling purpose. Audacious is you insisting that no material circumstance can interfere with your ability to shine the light of your spiritual nature.

In the field of audacity, our electricity is noticeable. We dazzle and shimmer, sparkle and shine—literally, our positive spiritual forwardness is contagious! We light up a dark room. We inspire others. We bless the world.

Devotion

The Gospel of Thomas contains many parallels to the four Gospels familiar to Christians worldwide. Scholars today date the writing of Thomas as early as fifty years after Jesus, which suggests that Thomas may have been a source for the later

Gospel writers. In Thomas, as in the canonized four, Jesus is known to have made some radical statements, provocative if not downright heretical. Among my favorites is this:

> His disciples questioned him: Should we fast? In what way should we pray? Should we give to charity? From which foods should we abstain? Jesus responded: Do not lie. If there is something that you hate, do not do it, for everything is revealed beneath heaven. Nothing hidden will fail to be displayed. Nothing covered will remain undisclosed (Thomas 6).

Don't you just love indirect answers? Can't you just imagine Jesus, with a twinkle in his eye, giving the disciples not a simple answer but one that springs from the intent behind the question? Turning Jesus' answers into positive statements, we may glean this meaning: Tell the truth; be in integrity with yourself. Do what you love for the love of it—be unified—which was Jesus' primary message throughout Thomas, to be *one*, to know our Divine Identity. Jesus seems to be reminding us that whatever our inner motivation, it will come out. I like to say, "character reveals itself."

A little further along in the Gospel of Thomas, as if finally answering the questions posed in Logion 6, Jesus says: "If you fast, you will give rise to sin for yourselves; and if you pray, you will be condemned; and if you give alms, you will do harm to your spirits" (Thomas 14a).

Traditionally, the role of fasting, praying, and charitable acts in Judaism (and in other faith traditions) had been almost superstitious: Do these practices to become worthy, to get God's approval—and therefore God's intervention—and to become "holy" or "sanctified." In his customary way, Jesus startled his listeners by using reverse psychology, of sorts. Imagine how the disciples may have received this instruction—surely Jesus would not advocate eliminating the foundational practices of their faith! Perhaps Jesus was suggesting that the error would be to fast, pray, and give to charity as a means to achieve God's favor or to qualify for God's love. Perhaps Jesus is inviting a more authentic spiritual activity arising from awareness of our Divine Identity such that our practices reflect our devotion.

Devotion is our capacity for wholehearted, single-minded attention. It is our power of intensity, the fire in our belly. As an aspect of zeal, devotion fulfills the law of mind, which is: where thought goes, energy flows. The flow of energy responding to devoted attention is not random; it is precise, amplifying and reproducing the original thought. This is why spiritual practice is essential for a spiritual experience of life. Practice builds up our consciousness so that achieving desired states of equanimity and unity becomes easier, as well as speedier, as consciousness blossoms.

A young man seeks a famous martial artist with whom to study. The young man tells the master of his desire to become the best martial artist in the world. He asks the master, "How long will I need to study?" The master answers, "Ten years at least." The young man thinks ten years would be far too long. "How long if I really applied myself and studied harder than any other student?" asks the prospective student. "Twenty years," replied the master. The young man, perplexed about why working harder could double his time in study, understood the master's explanation: "When one eye is fixed upon your destination, there is only one eye left with which to find the way."

Devotion is present-moment engagement. Zeal is wasted when directed toward an arrival point in the future, because zeal can only be experienced in the present moment. Enthusiasm, audacity, and devotion press *toward* the future, but it is necessary to live in the present in order to get to the future. Appreciation of the moment's possibilities grounds us in zeal. We can appreciate our future potential while living consciously in the now.

Meditation for Zeal

As I begin to relax and concentrate, I gently stretch my upper shoulders and neck. Slowly I rotate my head, beginning chin to chest and moving in the direction of left ear, then chin to chest, then right ear. Breathing in and out intentionally, softening. Inhaling, I lift my shoulders toward my ears, hold posture and breath, then release and become still.

I direct my full attention to the back of my neck, at the top of my cervical spinal cord. Here, where the lower brain stem, or medulla oblongata, connects to my brain and spinal cord lies the center of my spiritual power of zeal. The medulla oblongata controls important autonomic functions such as breathing, blood pressure, and heart rate. I visualize a vibrant orange glow permeating the back of my neck and deep within my brain. I send the message "relax" to my brain, and sense the slowing of breath and pulse as I still my body and quiet my mind.

I AM the magnificent power of zeal. I am enthusiastic, audacious, and devoted. I eagerly awaken each morning on purpose, exuberant about the choices ahead of me. I boldly think, envision, and act in the direction of my intentions. I devote my thought, energy, and time toward being a blessing by using my gifts and talents for good. I AM the ever-flowing, always forward-moving vibration of possibility. I remain attentive to the present moment, knowing that my focus on the present is my ticket to my desired future.

I am centered in the evolutionary divine power of zeal, an inexhaustible supply of passion and readiness. I do not dissipate this power by empty or frenetic activity; instead, I remain wholehearted and single-minded in my spiritual practice of enthusiasm, audacity, and devotion. I am inspired and focused, exhilarated in my sense of purpose.

Practices to Cultivate Zeal

1. Read the Meditation for Zeal daily, or make an audio recording and listen to it daily. Choose one of the affirmations in the meditation to recite and contemplate.

2. Write about zeal in your journal. Here are some questions you might choose to reflect upon:

   - What are some qualitative differences between the power of enthusiasm and anxious or frenetic energy? Identify some markers for you that let you know when you are in one state or the other.

   - What is worth waking up for each day?

   - Remember a time when someone labeled you "pushy" or "arrogant." Or, remember a time when you labeled someone else "pushy" or "arrogant." How does substituting the word "audacious" as it is defined in this section reveal a passion underneath the behavior?

- Recall one project or endeavor to which you were devoted. Write about the quality of the time you devoted to it. Describe how you felt when absorbed in the details.

3. Create or select a symbol for zeal to display where you will see it often. Here are some examples: a candle; an image of a hot air balloon; an original drawing, collage, or sculpture.

4. Practice the Kundalini Yoga Breath of Fire, a breathing exercise featuring rhythmic inhalations and exhalations through the nostrils while pumping the abdomen. Search online for written instructions and video demonstrations.

6

THE LIGHT OF POWER— THE POWER OF CONCENTRATION, SELF-MASTERY, AND AUTHORITY

Then God said, "Let us make humankind in our image, according to our likeness; and let them have dominion over the fish of the sea, and over the birds of the air, and over the cattle, and over all the wild animals of the earth, and over every creeping thing that creeps upon the earth."

—Genesis 1:26

All authority in heaven and on earth has been given to me.

—Matthew 28:18

The Power that rules the world is within.

—Charles Fillmore, *Atom-Smashing Power of Mind*

WHEN I WAS LITTLE, MY electrician Dad taught my six brothers and sisters and me that we had the power to flip a switch and make the lights come on or go off. Dad rigged up all kinds of magic switches in our house, having us believe that by blowing our breath on a certain Christmas tree ornament, we would cause the lights to brighten or change color. Dad had us clapping our hands to turn the electric fireplace on and off years before "the clapper" went on the market. Again and again, we would be amazed at our power to manipulate lights.

We were created for power. It's in us to succeed, to move forward, and to accomplish. As is true for all our abilities, power can be used to improve or control our material life, and it can be cultivated as spiritual power for inner transformation as well as for blessing others. A hundred years ago, Charles Fillmore captured the trouble so many have in succeeding: "Today men are striving to acquire power through money, legislation, and man-made government, and falling short because they have not mastered themselves" (*The Twelve Powers of Man*, 67).

A familiar affirmation in Unity communities is "There is only one Power in the universe, God/Good" (H. Emilie Cady, *Lessons in Truth*, 44). God is not a being that expresses power. God is power itself; we are the divine power expressing powerfully. We express our power ability in the following ways.

Concentration

A fan of the NBA's San Antonio Spurs, I marveled during the 2012 NBA Western Conference finals at how suddenly the game can change. Repeatedly during the series between the Spurs and the Oklahoma City Thunder, one team would go on a run, succeeding at both ends of the court, dazzling fans with their speed and team play, and rapidly outscoring their opponents. Out of nowhere, in the blink of an eye, the energy of the game would shift as the opposing team swallowed up their contender's lead. It happened again in the 2013 Western Conference finals when the Spurs bested the Memphis Grizzlies, and the NBA finals when the Miami Heat took the championship. Thrilling basketball! Metaphysician that I am, I curiously considered the phenomenon in view of our spiritual abilities. Whenever a team member heightened his concentration, the intensifying effect of his focus spread through the team, not verbally but vibrationally. We can, by harnessing our concentration ability, turn our inner defeatism toward optimism.

Concentration is the opposite of and antidote for multitasking, with its false promise of increasing achievement. We cannot multitask; we can only focus on one thing at a time. Attempts to multitask lead to rapid switching from one focus to another, reducing our attention on anything and diminishing the quality of our focus. Our concentration ability is the power of single-mindedness. Concentration intensifies thought the way a laser intensifies light.

Researchers studying intelligence discovered that memory is less a factor in intelligence than "one's ability to control their selective attention" (www.howtogetfocused.com). Upon what, then, should we focus? David Eagleman, in his book *Incognito: The Secret Lives of the Brain*, stresses that concentration is tricky: hyper-focus on our actions actually diminishes our capacity to achieve. For example, as I discovered years ago taking timed typing tests for clerical assignments, our attention on every finger position on a keyboard greatly reduces our speed and increases our errors. In recent years, San Antonio Spurs player Tim Duncan improved his shooting from the foul line. His previous record at the line was pitiful in comparison to his true shooting ability. I would watch, squirming, as Tim would position himself at the line, take several breaths and phantom shots, and then stiffly raise his arms, let go, and hope the ball made it through the hoop. Most of the time, it did not due to Tim's hyper-focus on each of the postures and movements required for successful shooting—a complex series that, after training, must come seamlessly.

What, then, is the object of our focus? I believe Jesus' apostle Paul taught us in these words: "Finally, brothers {and sisters}, whatever is true, whatever is honorable, whatever is just, whatever is pure, whatever is lovely, whatever is commendable, if there is any excellence, if there is anything worthy of praise, think about these things" (Philippians 4:8). Each of "these things" points to an ideal found only in our truest Self, our Infinite Self, the source of which is divine— divine honor, divine justice, divine love. Direct attention to these divine attributes, and "You shall receive power when the Holy Spirit has come upon you" (Acts 4:8). "When you search for me, you will find me; if you seek me with all your heart" (Jeremiah 29:43). The object of our attention, the "me," is the I AM or spiritual Self, the holy, whole spirit of the divine that is our true nature.

Self-Mastery

Every religious discipline teaches it. Every culture values it. Self-control or self-mastery is a key to power:

Who is strong? He who controls his passions. (Judaism; Mishnah)

The strong man is not the good wrestler; the strong man is only he who controls himself when he is angry. (Islam; Hadith of Bukhari and Muslim)

He who conquers others has physical strength; he who conquers himself is strong. (Taoism; Tao Te Ching, Star, *Two Suns Rising*, 33)

Though one should conquer a million men on the battlefield, yet he, indeed, is the noblest victor who has conquered himself. (Buddhism; Dhammapada, 103)

With the conquest of my mind, I have conquered the whole world. (Sikhism; *World Scripture*, 522)

That man is disciplined and happy who can prevail over the turmoil that springs from desire and anger, here on earth. (Hinduism; *Bhagavad Gita* 5:23)

For God did not give us a spirit of cowardice, but rather a spirit of power and of love and of self-discipline. (Christianity; 2 Timothy 1:7)[2]

Note: The words "strong" and "strength" are used in some of these quotations because English language dictionaries name the words *strength* and *power* as synonyms. As addressed in these pages and in Charles Fillmore's teaching, strength and power are each distinct spiritual abilities.

Self-mastery is our capacity to guide our thoughts, words, and actions in integrity with our Infinite Self, instead

---

2 This collection of quotations from *World Scripture*, 522–23.

of reacting from only-human, or egoic, impulses. We know ourselves. We respect ourselves, and we respect others. We do not fool ourselves but tell ourselves the truth. We seek to understand the beliefs and attitudes underlying our impulsive emotions, so that we can correct misguided beliefs and change our attitudes, knowing our emotions will settle as we do so.

Self-mastery is a claiming of our wholeness and self-determination. When my children were toddlers, I swapped babysitting with another mom. One day, her child, unhappy with me because I did not allow him to do everything he wanted, cried out, "You are not the boss of me!" After I got over feeling stunned, I thought to myself, he is so right! I hope he knows this as he grows up. No one should be the boss of us, and nothing should have power over us. Yet in our misunderstanding of our rightful power ability, we give our power over to other people; we are controlled by our compulsions; and we operate from fixed attitudes. All of these are addressed by cultivating our power ability.

Early in my work of church ministry, an iridologist was scheduled to offer a workshop on a Sunday afternoon at the Unity church I was serving. The church was in transition, as was I, having been an associate to the minister who had recently departed for another church. My position was tenuous. I was the de facto spiritual leader with little training or experience. Into this scenario entered an iridologist eager to demonstrate his accuracy in reading the eyes to diagnose conditions of consciousness—and then in his workshop to teach his remedies. I knew nothing of iridology, or this man, when he approached me minutes ahead of the start of the first of two Sunday services that I was officiating. Casually, at the coffee station in the reception room, he looked into my eyes and told me, "You are insecure, and nervous. I could help you with that." I became speechless. I bolted out of the room and went to my office to attempt to compose myself. I fumbled through the first service, *insecure and nervous*. Afterward, the iridologist came and knocked on my office door, offering to teach me by example how to deliver a Sunday message that connects with people—obviously, I had done a poor job of it. In my deflated state, I agreed! Following the second service, a few lay leaders sensed something had gone wrong. After all, I was scheduled to deliver the message at both services. Protective of me, the lay leaders accosted the iridologist, who later apologized to me for being insensitive. He had only wanted to help.

This painful experience was revealing to me. First, the uncomfortable truth was that he had nailed me—he saw my insecurity and nervousness; if *he* could, so could others. I was a public mess, I believed! I told my husband Giles. In his wisdom, Giles advised, "When you respect yourself, others will respect you." Bingo! I began to see that calling myself a victim of another person's bullying, or domination, only meant that I had given over my power to him. I earnestly began to study self-mastery, over time learning to respect myself, to trust myself, and to be self-determining. I learned there is a difference between aggressiveness, the taming of which is central to the classic definition of self-mastery; and assertiveness, which is a healthy aspect of consciousness. I learned to assert myself deliberately and positively during uncomfortable interactions with others.

Some might say there are higher, more spiritual applications of our power ability than in minor interpersonal incidents. I believe, however, that all healthy expressions of our power ability are spiritual. Read advice columns such as "Dear Abby" or "Carolyn Hax" in your local newspaper and you'll likely agree that most of humanity's interpersonal struggles arise when we feel out of control, which we often translate as being under someone else's control. Some examples of classic power struggles might include the following:

You reside in the tropics. Relatives from the north like to visit. You routinely inconvenience yourself when relatives make vacation plans in your area, expecting you to host them in your home. You allow one relative to stay for a month. Another family offers to pay for nothing during their stay, accepting your hospitality, eating your food, and driving your car. Despite your negative feelings, when they call to schedule next year's vacation, you say yes! You can't help it—they're family.

A friend and you regularly schedule time together at local restaurants. Your friend determines which restaurant every time, and you go along even when you don't care for that restaurant's cuisine or the price range is beyond your means.

Your work involves collaboration with others. A coworker arrives late for meetings, contributes almost nothing to the project, takes credit for the key idea that you bring to the table, and is the first one to accept praise when the assignment has been accomplished. You can't correct the coworker because no one else seems to care, and you can't complain to the boss because you might appear petty.

Any or all of these situations would be reasonable and acceptable if you genuinely felt hospitable, acquiescent, and gracious. Implied in each of these accounts, however, is the sense that you feel disgruntled but unable to assert yourself. Others are in control. Others control you.

Why is it important to cultivate self-mastery in these seemingly small matters? I believe that everyday power struggles lead to rifts, family feuds, and wars! Everyday power struggles lead to self-degradation and deflation of self-worth, which lead to your dimming your inner light and withdrawing from being the blessing you are here on earth to be.

If you are the unhappy host, Abby and Carolyn might advise you to become proactive with your family. Let them know they are welcome for up to four days at a time; send them lists of local hotels and rental-car companies, etc.; and be truthful if someone's scheduled visit interferes with your already-scheduled plans. If you are the friend who never expresses your opinion, the advice columnists might urge you to find your voice or to take the lead and suggest your preference. If you are the frustrated coworker, advisors might recommend you begin with a one-on-one, heart-to-heart visit with the underperforming team member.

Any remedies for situations of perceived powerlessness involve claiming our power ability. Consider this: Whenever we have an issue with another person, ignoring it or sidestepping it is an act of disrespect. We disrespect the other person by telling ourselves they couldn't handle our honest feedback. Telling ourselves "it's not that big a deal" or "I'll get over it," we disrespect ourselves.

Cultivating self-mastery along with the courage of our strength ability, we become self-knowing, transparent, and confident—and we sleep better at night.

Another expression of self-mastery is overcoming compulsive behaviors. I remember at the age of twenty-one, having smoked cigarettes for four years, I was driving to work one winter morning. Windows were up, heat was on. Cigarette smoke was swirling in such a thick cloud that I could hardly see through the windshield. I was coughing and having trouble breathing. In a flash of awareness, I realized, *Cigarettes have taken control! They intrude when I drink my cup of coffee first thing in the morning, after every meal, at my break during the workday, whenever I have a telephone chat with a friend, before I go to bed. I don't have cigarettes. Cigarettes have me!* I extinguished my lit cigarette and threw the rest of the pack out the car window.

Jesus said, "Whatever you bind on earth will be bound in heaven; and whatever you loose on earth shall be loosed in heaven" (Matthew 18:18). I find two helpful ways of interpreting this master teaching. First, I think of earth as the microcosm and heaven as the macrocosm. Quantum physics is proving the holographic nature of life, meaning that all parts are contained in each part. An action taken in one small part affects the whole. This is why master teachers of all ages have advised that if we were to commit to one modest practice toward conscious living, we—in entirety—would awaken.

Another way of interpreting Jesus' profound statement is to understand *earth* means you, your body and your circumstances; *heaven* means your spirit and *the* spirit in unity with all, or oneness. Charles Fillmore taught that when you bind or control "the appetites, passions, and emotions in the body {earth}," you simultaneously establish your power in subtle, vibrational, spiritual matters; thereby, "you restore equilibrium between heaven and earth, or Spirit and matter" (*The Twelve Powers of Man*, 69).

The second of the Ten Commandments Charlton Heston brought down from Mount Sinai—rather, Moses (wanted to be sure you are with me), instructs—"You shall not make for yourself an idol" (Exodus 20:4). In King James Version, *idol* is "a graven image." An idol or graven image means one that is carved.

My dad used to say, "After laughing comes crying." This phrase was similar to other adages such as "the other shoe is about to drop" and "all good things come to an end."

I verified this truism in my experience in the early years of my marriage. Our household income at that time barely exceeded our expenses. I would deposit a little money each month in a savings account. I would feel good about getting ahead. Then, just as I had come to expect, one of a gazillion car parts would break or a pair of eyeglasses would get sat upon, and I would have to empty the account and go back to zero savings. I lived with a perpetual sense of impending dread. The better I was feeling one minute, the bigger the next minute's dread.

By acquiescing to my dad's repeated adage, I was worshipping a graven image. I had fixed in my consciousness a belief that was played out in my experience repeatedly. We give our power over to false beliefs when we claim "my diabetes" or "my allergies." We can never heal these fleeting conditions by believing them to be permanent. Uncovering our fixed attitudes about life and, especially, about ourselves, releases our inner power of self-mastery. Unity leader Eric Butterworth wrote:

> We also hold fixed false attitudes (graven images) about ourselves—I am weak, not as smart as . . . worthless, unlovable, incapable . . . "To be created

in the image of God" means that "in the beginning" (in principle) you were formed as an idea in Infinite Mind. You can never be less than the God-idea in expression . . . You do not need a new self-image. What you need is to let go of the graven image of yourself that you have carved into the fabric of your subconscious mind, and to know and release your own divine image (Butterworth, *Breaking the Ten Commandments*, 25-26).

Spiritual Authority

A tradition in Unity communities is singing "Let There Be Peace on Earth" at the conclusion of Sunday services. Written by Jill Jackson Miller and Sy Miller in 1955, the lyrics inspire us to know that "peace begins with me." Over the years, Unity congregations have modestly altered the lyrics; for example, changing "let me walk with my brothers" to "let me walk with my family" or "let us walk with each other." I was surprised when I heard one congregation singing, "Yes, there is peace on earth and yes it begins with me." I thought, perhaps they do not understand the power of "let there be!"

"Let there be" and "let me be" are not pleas for another power, God, to act or cause us to act. Rather, they are an inward call for spiritual authority. It is not a request, but a command. It is a powerful assertion of authority. It is the cry of the creator—"Let there be light!"—and it is our creative self-command to some spiritual ability—"Let me be the light!"

Going into a hospital room for a pastoral visit, or walking to the front of the church to begin Sunday services, I live into the command "Let there be . . ." Clergy in many religious communities wear liturgical robes signifying the mantle, or cloak, of spiritual authority. I do not wear robes, but I shift into a consciousness of spiritual service. I energetically cloak myself with spiritual authority. I sense the distinction between my human personality and my Infinite Self or Divine Identity directed into service. I reduce my focus on my personality, which means I turn my attention away from myself—for example my attire or concern about forgetting to say something important. I become completely interested in what is important, what will uplift, what will provoke, and what will inspire. I become interested in *presence*.

The Gospel accounts of Jesus portray his spiritual authority. It was Jesus' presence, more than his words, by which people caught a glimpse of their true nature and relieved themselves of terrible conditions. Jesus glowed. The woman who reached for his cloak, believing that touching it would heal her, did not depend upon Jesus' words but his presence. He stood solidly divine. She reached into Jesus' Divine Identity to glimpse her own Divine Identity.

Jesus' spiritual authority came not from his personality and not from his intellect. His authority came "from the Father"—his source of inner wisdom. We, too, must partner power with wisdom in order to be centered in spiritual truth.

You don't have to become a minister to assert spiritual authority. You can visit a friend or relative in the hospital and be the cloak they touch. You can be a presence so solidly standing in the truth of wholeness that your loved one feels empowered to experience her wholeness and well-being while undergoing medical care.

You can be the truth teller in your family, your work-place, and community. When people in your presence display discouragement, you can encourage them with the truth of their Divine Identity. When they express worry about money, you can remind them of the blessings all around them. When they fret over an illness, you can spark their inner knowing of their wholeness of being.

In matters of opinion, you express humanly. In matters of ultimate truth, discover that truth within you and express it with spiritual authority.

Meditation for Power

Through my breath I sense the power of this present moment. I breathe intentionally, fully, a whole-body breath energizing my entire body. I breathe this way for several minutes, until I sense the concentration of spiritual power in my throat chakra.

The root of the tongue, or the throat chakra, is the seat of spiritual power. I bathe this area with the color of bright purple, a healing stream of light.

I AM the power of concentration, self-mastery, and spiritual authority. My source of power is divine power.

By my divine nature, I cannot be powerless or ill. I am not in the world to cower in the presence of others' power. I release any hesitancy to shine the full light of spiritual aware-ness in the world.

All power is mine in heaven and on earth—in spiritual as well as material aspects of life. By spiritual power, I concentrate on shining the light of love, life, wisdom, and all spiritual pow-ers into my life and into the world. I AM master of my thoughts, words, and actions. I master myself, respect myself, and hold myself accountable. By spiritual power, I AM a presence in whose presence other people awaken to their Divine Identity.

Practices to Cultivate Power

1. Read the Meditation for Power daily, or make an audio recording and listen to it daily. Choose one of the affirmations in the meditation to recite and contemplate.

2. Write about power in your journal. Here are some questions you might choose to reflect upon:

   • Concentrate your attention on an ideal you value: world peace, compassion, etc. In what ways have you observed this ideal being expressed in the world? How do *you* express this ideal in your life?

   • When is it best to hold your tongue and when is it best to speak your mind? Describe occasions when you have done one but later wished you had done the other.

   • Write about the importance of your presence to your loved ones. What qualities do they see in you that they rely upon during times of challenge?

   • Recall your experience of speaking with spiritual authority—a time when you did not consciously construct your words of encouragement or guidance but they seemed to arise from a greater wisdom. What impact did your words have on the other person? On you?

3. Create or select a symbol for power to display where you will see it often. Here are some examples: a megaphone; an

image of a lightning bolt; an original drawing, collage, or sculpture.

4. Develop spiritual power through the meditation practice of mantra, repeatedly reciting or singing an affirmation or scripture verse in any language. Vocalization supports the development of power by stimulating the throat chakra, the power center in the body.

7

THE LIGHT OF LOVE—
THE POWER OF MAGNETISM,
HARMONY, AND UNITY

God is Love and those who abide in Love, abide in God and God abides in them.

—1 John 4:16

God does not love anybody or anything. God is the love in everybody and everything. God is love; man becomes loving by permitting that which God is to find expression in word and act.

—Charles Fillmore, *Jesus Christ Heals*

The individual suffers because he perceives duality. Find the One everywhere and in everything and there will be an end to pain and suffering.

—Sri Anandamayi Ma

WHILE VISITING AFTER THE FUNERAL of my paternal grand-mother and aunt, who died of heart attacks five minutes apart in two different hospitals, my cousin remarked that her one desire had always been to hear her mother tell her "I love you." Interestingly, it had been an issue for me growing up as well, which is why my cousin's statement grabbed my attention. My father, the source of *my* issue, cleared up the matter for us by explaining that people born in his and his sister's generation would have never said "I love you" to their child. "I love you" was reserved for your sweetheart. "I love you" spoken to your child would have seemed emotionally incestuous. It must have been in the free love years, then, the sixties, that "I love you" became popular in Western culture for all kinds of relationships, including nonhuman ones: "I love my sweetheart." "I love my kids." "I love my pets." "I love chocolate."

The overused word *love* is much misunderstood. Mis-understood love is behind unspeakable acts such as phys-ical and sexual abuse: "It's because I love you so much." Love is too often used as a weapon: "I'll love you if you will do what I ask you"; "I will withdraw love if you do not." People say, "I love you" to get sex and material gifts. Every day, three or more women and one man are murdered by their "sweethearts" in fits of jealousy or rage provoked by love.

When love is understood as merely a feeling—affection, desire, attachment, or devotion—it makes sense that love can get warped. Affection, desire, attachment, and devotion turn to obsession in an unhealthy mind.

If not a feeling, what, then, is love? Love is a universal power: the power of magnetism, harmony, and unity, as Erich Fromm tells us:

> Love is not primarily a relationship to a specific person; it is an attitude, an orientation of character that determines the relatedness of a person to the world as a whole, not toward one "object" of love . . . Yet, **most people believe that love is constituted by the object, not by the faculty.** In fact, *they even believe that it is proof of the intensity of their love when they do not love anybody except the "loved" person* . . . Because one does not see that **love is an activity, a power of the soul**,[3] one believes that all that is necessary to find is the right object—and that everything goes by itself afterward. This attitude can be compared to that of a man who wants to paint but who, instead of learning the art, claims that he has just to wait for the right object, and that he will paint beautifully when he finds it (Fromm, *The Art of Loving*, 46).

Magnetism

And I, when I am lifted up from the earth, will draw all people to myself.

—John 12:32

....

3 Bolded emphasis mine.

Gravity causes objects in the universe to be drawn to one another. Gravity operates in the macrocosm—birthing new heavenly bodies and then keeping them in orbit. In the microcosm, gravity ensures that Newton's apple falls to the ground, every time, and supports the body's cardiovascular system and other organs.

Two of science's great minds disagreed about the definition of gravity. Newton's gravity is a force that draws all objects to one another. Einstein's gravity is a distortion or curve in the shape of space-time. Although experts agree gravity does not produce a magnetic field in the way a common magnet does, gravity is the drawing power in the material world.

"Love is the drawing power of the mind" (Fillmore, *Talks on Truth*, 55). It is impersonal—has no particular object—and is universal—it shines like the sun shines, on all in its path. Love's magnetizing power attracts me to people and situations that reflect harmony and unity as well as those that appear to *repel* harmony and unity. Understanding this is understanding the law of attraction, which is based upon the principle and power of love.

In college, I dated a young man named Dale. The first time he invited me to his house, where he lived with his parents, Dale warned me that his mother would probably behave civilly but not warmly toward me. He explained that he was his mother's only living child, his brother having died a few years earlier, and she was protective and possessive of him.

Sure enough, Dale's mother did not warm to me, and she turned a cold shoulder to me time and again over many months. One morning Dale called to tell me his father had

had a heart attack and was hospitalized. I thought about what I could do to be supportive. I did what I had observed my mother do for friends and family. I purchased a pie and brought it to Dale's mother, at her house. When I arrived, Dale was not at home. I had timed it that way, in hopes of being alone with his mother. Dale's mother appeared surprised to find me at her door and carrying a pie. She let me in and offered me a chair. She sat across from me, seeming uncomfortable at first. I cannot recall my words, or hers, but I do recall that Dale's mother warmed to me during our first conversation alone together. She shared from her heart with me, revealing some of her hopes and worries for her family. She appeared grateful for and emotionally affected by my visit.

From that time forward, Dale's mother adored me and doted on me. Months later, when I stopped dating Dale, his mother blamed him and felt a sense of loss.

The change of heart Dale's mother experienced with me, and my own awakening to the magnetizing power of love, have stayed with me through the years. I believe that her attempts to protect and possess her son, and to distance herself from others, stemmed from the sorrow Dale's mother felt in having loved and lost. She had little reason to trust love after her child's death. She felt even more vulnerable when her husband suffered a heart attack. Yet, love is what she was made of. Love drew her toward me. Love drew me to her, as well. I felt inexplicably, urgently driven to extend myself to her, to reach her, to connect with her.

Although the law of attraction is often implied when we run into circumstances that we would label negative, I believe the highest law of attraction is love. The magnetizing power of love is our true nature, in which we can rightly claim, I AM Love: "And I, when I am lifted up from the earth, will draw all people to myself "(John 12:32). The good news about the law of attraction is that love, the great magnet, is what pulls us in *every* circumstance, good and bad. Situations are not being sent our way by some *other* source. We, as love, go into all circumstances. We attract ourselves into the details of our life, for love. The light of love wants to shine, to heal, to transform, to unify, and to harmonize.

Harmony

> *Above all, clothe yourself with love, which binds everything together in perfect harmony.*

> —Colossians 3:14

> *We know that all things work together for good for those who love God, who are called according to his purpose.*

> —Romans 8:28

Love is capable of unconditional acceptance and the view "All things work together for good." "Those who love God," in the above referenced scripture, may be understood as those who draw from the source of love, those who are focused upon the power of love. Charles Fillmore said about the power of love, "It insists that all is good, and by refusing to see anything but good it causes that quality finally to appear uppermost in itself and in all things" (*Talks on Truth*, 60).

Looking for the good in all circumstances is a timeless and cross-cultural spiritual instruction, as illustrated in this classic tale from India:

> A king has a loyal advisor who has an annoying habit of responding to each event by saying "That is Good." He says this when the king loses his toe in a hunting accident. The king fires him from his job. Some months later the king is captured by a group of tribesmen who plan to use him in a sacrificial ceremony. On discovering that his toe is gone, they declare him unfit as he has "already been cut." The tribesmen let the king go. Once he is safely back in the palace he calls the advisor to him and reinstates him in his job. "You were right," he said, "It was good that I lost my toe for it saved my life today. But why did you say it was good when I fired you from your job?" The advisor answered. "Your Highness, I cannot see the future, but I have learned to trust that some good comes from each event. Today I see what that was for me. For as you recall I was loyal to you, and had you not fired me, I would have remained with you when you were captured by the tribesmen. And because I am in possession of all my fingers and toes, I would have been next in line for the sacrifice!" (Pearmain, *Doorways to the Soul*).

It may be challenging for us to truly hold the position that good can be found in everyone and in all things. Easy when people and things look lovely; daunting when people and things appear unlovely. Although the only-human tendency is to highlight the bad, the wrong, and the worst, our spiritual nature naturally points out the good. In the aftermath of human tragedies such as the 2012 Sandy Hook Elementary School shooting resulting in the deaths of twenty-six people (twenty of them children) and the 2012 Hurricane Sandy, which caused nearly three hundred deaths and massive physical damage, amidst the cries of sorrow we heard stories of heroism and appreciation. My sister and brother-in-law's beach house on a barrier island in New Jersey incurred significant damage, and with interest I followed my brother-in-law's updates on Facebook for weeks after the storm. I was moved day after day learning of neighbors assisting one another and the spirit of the community rising to rebuild "in unity." People who had cause to feel ruined expressed gratitude for their capacity to create anew.

Even as we abhor the actions of mass murderers and terrorists, we seek to understand. Amid cries for justice we hear calls for compassion. We know that a person has to feel alone, disconnected, and disturbed to maim and kill others. We discuss how to ensure better mental health care and to limit ownership of guns as ways of restoring harmony.

The harmonizing power of love is natural to us. Within us, at the core of us, is a set point for interpreting life's people and events in the direction of *good*. As the late great Unity leader Eric Butterworth taught, we are "not in the world to set it right but to see it rightly" (*Discover the Power Within You*, 68). Nowhere is this evidenced more than in the valiant effort we make to resolve discord in our lives. We have a built-in intolerance for disharmony. Signals of discord arise from within us— from discordant thoughts and feelings, even when it appears the discord is outside of us, in the world around us or in a particular circumstance. Fortunately, the ability to restore harmony is also innate.

When your automobile collides with another on the road, no matter how inconvenient or troublesome, you don't pull away only to smash into the other car over and over again. No, you pull away and then seek to restore harmony.

When you are driving down an unfamiliar road and come to orange barriers indicating the road ahead is closed, no matter how frustrated you may feel you do not crash into the barrier and curse at it for being in your way. No, you back up and find another way to get where you are going—restoring harmony.

When you collect your groceries and get to the checkout counter only to discover you left your wallet at home, no matter how upset you may feel you do not start screaming at the clerk as if the clerk is at fault. You don't get mad at your wallet for abandoning you. You do whatever is most appropriate to restore harmony, whether it's returning to the store to pay for your groceries or moving ahead to another planned activity.

The harmonizing power of love within us is our capacity for harmonious thoughts, words, and actions regarding others and ourselves. I remember many times early in my marriage when Giles and I would zig and zag (our description for disagreeing). I could not go to sleep at night without talking it out. I would lie in bed replaying the situation, justifying my disharmonious feelings, thinking I was right or worrying I was wrong, stewing in my discomfort, until I shot out of bed and insisted that we talk it over. Trouble was, Giles processes disharmony differently from me. Giles needs time. The gift of Giles's temperament to me was an opportunity for me to seek inward restoration of harmony. I learned to tap the source of love within. I learned to trust the harmonizing power of love, first within me and then within my relationship.

Unity

> *The glory that you have given me I have given them, so that they may be one, as we are one, I in them and you in me, that they may become completely one . . .*

> —John 17:24

> *Blessed are they that are One within themselves. They will find the Kingdom.*

> —Gospel of Thomas 49

We are One. One with God. One with all others. The essential unity of all is a truth discerned by mystics of all traditions in all times. A Course in Miracles teaches, "Heaven is not a place or a condition. It is merely an awareness of perfect oneness." Despite the truth of oneness, we humans often feel separate. Albert Einstein wrote, "Our separation of each other is an optical illusion of consciousness." Yet, "The experience of separateness arouses anxiety; it is, indeed, the source of all anxiety" (Fromm, *The Art of Loving*, 8).

The unifying power of love is the remedy for separation-consciousness.

The unifying power of love is our capacity for communion, empathy, and compassionate service. We see ourselves in one another.

The historic St. Francis of Assisi and contemporary Hindu *sadhus* (ascetic holy men) share a common attribute.

Poisonous snakes and wild animals, which have killed thousands of people every year, become docile in their presence. It is said that birds have built nests in their hair as they have sat in meditation.

> Those who see all creatures within themselves
> And themselves in all creatures know no fear.
> Those who see all creatures in themselves
> And themselves in all creatures know no grief.
> How can the multiplicity of life
> Delude the one who sees its unity?
> (Isha Upanishad 6-7, *World Scripture*, 416)

Meditation for Love

I focus my attention on the energy center of love within my body, in and around my heart. To attune to this radiating center of love, I place my hands over my heart while envisioning a soft pink glow emanating from my heart.

Divine love is my name and true nature. I gratefully acknowledge that the well of love can never run dry, for the source of love is eternal. Under the influence of love, I awaken to more love than I have ever known.

I call forth the magnetizing power of divine love. My thoughts are magnetic. Whatever dreams I am holding, I send through them the pink light of love. I center myself in realization that the dreams I have planted and I am devoted to must bear fruit by the magnetizing power of love.

I call forth from within me the harmonizing power of love. Love harmonizes my thoughts, words, and actions so that I see things rightly and bring about good. I see myself, others, and all conditions through the lens of harmonizing love. I express love by seeing the good in all. I AM the harmonizing power of love.

I call forth from within me the unifying power of love. I AM divine love, unifying my thoughts, words, and actions until I know only oneness. I see myself in others, others in myself, and GOD in us all. For I AM One. I send out from within me the pink light of love, blessing me and all people and all of life.

I AM the power of love, loving.

Practices to Cultivate Love

1. Read the Meditation for Love daily, or make an audio recording and listen to it daily. Choose one of the affirmations in the meditation to recite and contemplate.

2. Write about love in your journal. Here are some questions you might choose to reflect upon:

   • In your understanding, how is love as a spiritual power different from love as a human emotion?

   • Describe how "love is the highest law of attraction" in your present circumstances.

   • Remember a time when a situation appeared bleak but you insisted on mining the good from it. What good came from your insistence?

   • How do you tend to behave when you perceive you are separate—meaning different—from others? How do you tend to behave when you perceive you are united with others?

3. Create or select a symbol for love to display where you will see it often. Here are some examples: a pink heart; a magnet; an original drawing, collage, or sculpture.

4. Give your time in loving service at a nonprofit organization of your choice, such as the food bank or animal shelter.

~~~

8

~~~

THE LIGHT OF WISDOM—
THE POWER OF JUDGMENT,
DISCERNMENT, AND INTUITION

*Get wisdom; get insight: do not forget, nor turn away from the
words of my mouth. Do not forsake her, and she will keep you; love
her, and she will guard you. The beginning of wisdom is this: Get
wisdom, and whatever else you get, get insight. Prize her highly,
and she will exalt you; she will honor you if you embrace her.*

—Proverbs 4:5–8

Do not judge by appearances, but judge with right judgment.

—John 7:24

*And when you turn to the right or when you turn to the left,
your ears shall hear a word behind you, saying, "This is the
way; walk in it."*

—Isaiah 30:21

WISDOM, LIKE ALL OUR SPIRITUAL abilities, is inborn. Wisdom expresses as a conscious level of functioning compared to instinct, which is not volitional but based on biological intelligence. Wisdom is often compared to knowledge. Knowledge, however, is our recall of information accumulated and stored in our brains. Knowledge is based on experience as well as study. It relies upon our capacity to sift through stored information in ways that form connections and reach conclusions. Wisdom is *applied* knowledge, our decision-making capacity through mental evaluation, spiritual discernment, and moment-by-moment intuition.

In Judeo-Christian traditions, wisdom is of such importance that it has been personified. The Hebrew word for "wisdom" is *hokhmah* (or *chokma*), related in feminine terms through Hebrew wisdom literature: "Say to wisdom, 'You are my sister'" (Proverbs 7:4); for wisdom "is better than jewels, and all that you may desire cannot compare with her" (Proverbs 8:11). In Greek, Sophia is the personification of wisdom. Gnostics portrayed Sophia as the energy of spiritual intuition—a partner with the creative principle in bringing the world into form.

The Christian New Testament introduces a masculine aspect of wisdom, the Holy Spirit. Early on, in the Jesus birth narratives, the Holy Spirit is represented much as it is in Judaism, as the pouring out of the divine into its creation where it then resides. The dwelling of GOD in humanity is represented in one Hebrew word: Shekinah (or Shechina), which is the feminine name for God in Judaism. Later in the Jesus story, the Holy Spirit becomes characterized as divine wisdom in masculine form: "But the Advocate, the Holy Spirit, whom the Father will send in my name, will teach you everything, and remind you of all that I have said to you" (John 14:26). Wisdom is so important that the Holy Spirit is the third in the Christian divine trinity.

Our wisdom ability is applicable in body, mind, and spirit—in every dimension of living:

> In the body, conclusions are reached through experience; in intellect, reason is the assumed arbiter of every question; in Spirit, intuition and inspiration bring the quick and sure answer to all the problems of life (Fillmore, *The Twelve Powers of Man*, 45).

Many writings about our spiritual capacities hint that expression in the body and intellect are somehow inferior to spiritual expression. I believe that wisdom is most potent, and effective, when integrated through all aspects of consciousness. The power of wisdom (and all our spiritual abilities) expressed physically and mentally builds our capacity; and as we practice expressing wisdom in these areas of life, we discover that intuition—our finest spiritual expression of wisdom—is involved in every decision we make. How could it not be? For we are not three distinct dimensions—we are one! Viewed in truth, every dimension of consciousness is spiritual.

Judgment

The original name for the power of wisdom, assigned by Charles Fillmore, was judgment. The word *judgment* fell out of use during the late twentieth century, however, because "to judge" smacked of judgmentalness and was confused with Bible literalists' divine judgment. The dictionary definition of *judgment* perfectly describes the aspect of wisdom relating to sound judgment, including our capacity to assess or evaluate situations and reach conclusions.

We judge every day. Charles Fillmore tells us, "Judgment is the mental act of evaluation through comparison or contrast" (Fillmore, *The Revealing Word*, 113). It is fundamental to the decision-making process. As a mental skill, judging or evaluating is clarifying. I am pretty sure I was born with the judging gene. From my earliest memory, I liked almost nothing better than to run a vertical line down the center of a blank piece of paper, labeling the top left column "pro" and the other column "con." I used this technique for deciding which summer camp to attend, whether to break up with a boyfriend, and which job offer to accept.

Doesn't seem so spiritual, does it? But I am certain it *is* spiritual. Every time I activated the power of wisdom by evaluating options, I learned about what gave life to my spirit. I learned to clarify my thoughts. I learned it is all right—and in fact necessary—to choose. I learned I can trust myself, that I AM wise. Also, I learned that the mental exercise of evaluating is not the only or final expression of wisdom in decision-making. Other factors come into play, nonmental factors or intuitive factors that, together with considered thought, make for wise decision-making.

"The Day of Judgment" looms over literalists in Judaism, Islam, and Christianity. On that day, it is believed God, the deity, will render a final, eternal judgment, separating good-doers from evildoers. Those who have been judged "good" will enter the everlasting kingdom of heaven and the "evildoers" will be cast into the eternal fire of hell. Read allegorically, which many Bible scholars and metaphysicians endorse, this is our call to integrity in our expression of judgment. "The Day of Judgment" occurs every day, in self-evaluation.

Self-evaluation, at the heart of our wisdom ability, leads us to ask ourselves: What is the right thing for me to do? What of my true nature am I here to express in this situation? What is the truth underlying this appearance? What would I choose to do if I knew I was love, wisdom, strength (or any of my spiritual abilities)? What have I done that I would do differently next time?

We all have an innate capacity to judge rightly. It is often referred to as our conscience—think Disney's Jiminy Cricket who exhorts Pinocchio, "always let your conscience be your guide." Think about how, over the years, you have built up an inner knowing from your practice of the faculty of judgment. Think about how many of your responses to circumstances seem to come automatically after years of practicing integrity. Think about, too, the many errors in judgment that you have made, in the past, from which you have learned to tune your integrity meter.

You know when you have judged rightly, for you are in heaven—in a state of peace, harmony, and well-being.

Discernment

When I get hold of a divine idea, I see in my imagination the benefit of it and am inclined to get 'er going. This has gotten me into trouble a time or two, when I either moved fast enough that others could not catch up to my idea or the idea turned out not to be such a good one. This is why I appreciate people with discernment on my team. On my church board of trustees, for example, I value the voice of someone who knows not to get on the bandwagon before sensing what might be missing, what might be unintended consequences, who will be affected and needs to know in advance, and other critical considerations prior to changing *anything* at church. My team members would probably say I, too, have built discernment muscle over the years.

Discernment is generally equated with judgment, although it is a particular kind of perception, sensing *without* judgment, really. Discernment is the ability not to rely upon facts but upon principles in decision-making. In spiritual practice, discernment is exercised through a process that includes questioning, meditating, and envisioning while suspending judgment about any divine ideas generated. Spiritual communities follow discernment processes to determine communal values and priorities. Individuals practice discernment for self-discovery and ratification of their path ahead.

Another practice of discernment is to allow a question space and time to percolate underneath conscious thinking, allowing impressions, images, and meaning to arise naturally over time. The expression "live the question" is a good way to describe this practice. Starting early in June 1998, and again in June 2004, I underwent forty days of perpetual menstrual bleeding that were eventually stopped with acupuncture treatments. It seemed odd that I would experience such an irregularity two times, three years apart. The only connection I could make between these two segments of time was that each of my two children graduated from high school in June of these years. I sensed the connection during the second go-round: My womb was weeping, I gathered. I felt perplexed about my body's experience of grief that I had not consciously felt. I lived into the question of maternal grief, which over time led me to think about my identity outside of mother-hood, to grieve the conclusion of my childbearing years, to dream about my purpose into the future, and to liberate my spirit so that I could joyously anticipate life post child-rearing. Discernment over time led me to ministry, authorship, coaching, and expressing purpose in ways I could not have imagined while my children were young.

Intuition

Dr. T. Berry Brazelton, pediatrician and author of more than thirty books about child development and parenting, spoke in a 2005 radio interview on NPR's *All Things Considered*. Dr. Brazelton recalled observing a mother and child in a grocery store one day, years ago. The child was crying. The mother was swatting at the child, which—imagine!—did not quiet her child. Dr. Brazelton wanted to pin the mother's arms to her sides to save this child. Instead, he paused to ask himself, "What do I know about this child and this mom?" Softly, Dr. Brazelton approached the mother and said to her, "It sure is no fun when you have to take your little one shopping." Mom looked incredulous. She sat down on the floor and cried, relieved that someone understood her. By now the child had stopped crying. The doctor watched as the little one approached her mom, crawled into her lap, and wrapped her arms around her. Dr. Brazelton had asserted his intuitive power of wisdom with the question, "What do I know?"

In a flash of intuition, he knew how to calm the mother so that "mom could do what she most desires to do, to love that child" (National Public Radio Podcast, 2005).

Contrast Dr. Brazelton's effective intuition with my attempt, when I was a young mother, to help a little one in a similar situation. Giles and I were one movie through a double feature at the drive-in theater in Honolulu—back in the day! The time was 11:30 p.m. In the car next to ours, a toddler, locked into her car seat in the rear, was crying. Two adults, probably her parents, were sitting in the front seats. The woman was turning around and swatting at the child, saying, "Hush. Stop crying." This went on for a long while, and I grew angrier by the minute. I told Giles, "I have to do something about this." He recommended I not. I couldn't help it. I yelled out to the two adults, "That child doesn't need to be spanked; she needs to be home in bed, asleep!" The man yelled back at me that the matter was none of my business. Just as the man opened his car door to step out, Giles ripped off the speaker that had been hanging on our car window and dropped it to the ground. He turned the key in the ignition and raced out of the lot. By now I was sobbing, worried about that baby and not understanding why Giles was hurrying out of there. First, Giles said he was concerned about our safety. "What if this guy had a gun?" Second, and more pointed, he thought that the chances were the child would be treated *worse* after I had agitated his parents. I would have liked to have a do-over on that one. I had acted righteously but not wisely. Plenty of additional opportunities to practice this aspect of wisdom have come my way over the years, and practice has made for progress.

Intuition is our aha! and uh-oh! power. Moment by moment, we have access to our internal guidance system. As we practice right judgment/evaluation and discernment, we activate and become familiar with the methods by which our Infinite Self takes charge to express wisely. We may see images, feel an electric charge, or hear a directive such as "check the tires" or "walk away." We may suddenly, without contemplation, know what to do.

One of the most frequent questions asked about our wisdom ability is, "How can I tell whether my intuition is from GOD or it's just my own (human) thought?" Many answers have been given to this question. Mine is, if it leads me to a behavior that helps me sleep better at night, if it rises in purity rather than in a confusion of my feelings, chances are it's a wise course of action. Is it GOD? Is it me? Yes, it is, it is oneness.

Cultivate an awareness of oneness, the truth of our Divine Identity or Infinite Self.

Meditation for Wisdom

Begin focusing attention at your solar plexus, which lies mainly on the front of the aorta, where this primary artery enters the abdomen by passing down through the diaphragm—at the "pit of the stomach," and behind the stomach itself. Most of the nerves in this area belong to the autonomic nervous system, which operates beneath conscious awareness. The solar plexus is considered the other brain because of its nerve sensitivity.

Affirm: I shine a yellow light, like the midday sun, through the region of my solar plexus. I bathe my solar plexus and the area around it with the brilliance of divine wisdom.

I never need to worry about knowing the right thing to do. I do not judge by appearances but by right judgment. I do not rush to conclusions but discern the way to go.

Everything I need to know is within me. Divine wisdom is my spiritual name and nature. I can trust my aha! and uh-oh! wisdom moment by moment. I discern through divine wisdom my deep inner sense of direction. I trust and follow my inner voice of wisdom. I rest easy as, centered in spiritual integrity, I AM true. I activate the power of wisdom in my body, mind, and spirit. I assert wisdom to live in the heavenly state of harmony, peace, and well-being. My tuning to divine wisdom blesses me and all others. I AM the divine power of wisdom, wise.

Spread the yellow sunlight of wisdom throughout your body, penetrating your skin and radiating out into the world, like sunlight streaming over the earth.

Practices to Cultivate Wisdom

1. Read the Meditation for Wisdom daily, or make an audio recording and listen to it daily. Choose one of the affirmations in the meditation to recite and contemplate.

2. Write about wisdom in your journal. Here are some questions you might choose to reflect upon:

   - How do you know when you have judged rightly?

   - Reflect on a big decision you made in recent years. How much time did you devote to evaluating the plusses and minuses? What other factors were involved in your discernment?

- Identify an area of uncertainty in your present life experience. What might you do to "live the question"?

- Recall moments in your past when you clearly felt guided by intuition. When you trusted the guidance and acted on it, what happened? When you did not trust and did not act, what happened?

3. Create or select a symbol for wisdom to display where you will see it often. Here are some examples: an image of the sun; an angel figurine; an original drawing, collage, or sculpture.

4. Practice the classic yoga posture Cat/Cow Pose, or Marjaryasana/Bidalasana. On your hands and knees, place your hands under your shoulders and knees under your hips. Keep your head and neck relaxed and in a neutral position. Slowly exhale as you pull your abdominal muscles in toward your spine, rounding your back toward the ceiling and tucking your tailbone down. Gently drop your head. Inhale and release the pose, returning to the starting posture. Repeat the movements slowly, elongating each breath in and out. Allow the movement to flow from your solar plexus, your wisdom center. Search online for detailed instruction and a video demonstration of the pose.

9

THE LIGHT OF STRENGTH— THE POWER OF STABILITY, COURAGE, AND TENACITY

In returning and rest you shall be saved; in quietness and in trust shall be your strength.

—Isaiah 30:15

Be strong in the Lord and in the strength of his power.

—Ephesians 6:10

SPIRITUAL STRENGTH IS OUR CAPACITY to stand undaunted in the midst of shifting circumstances, to act courageously, and to stay the course.

The Bible story of David and Goliath provides a striking illustration of the strength faculty. The Israelites prepared for a battle against the Philistines. A Philistine warrior named

Goliath verbally sparred with the Israelites, terrifying them all with his massive presence:

> His height was six cubits and a span. He had a helmet of bronze on his head, and he was armed with a coat of mail; the weight of the coat was five thousand shekels of bronze. He had greaves of bronze on his legs and a javelin of bronze slung between his shoulders. The shaft of his spear was like a weaver's beam, and his spear's head weighed six hundred shekels of iron; and his shield-bearer went before him. (1 Samuel 17:4–7)

Clearly, Goliath was immense and mighty.

A boy, David, was too young and weak to join the battle. His job was to bring provisions to his older brothers at the battlefield. David, however, heard the boastful rants of Goliath challenging the Israelites to a one-on-one battle. To the chagrin of his family, David went to King Saul and offered himself to fight against Goliath. Saul said to David: "You are not able to go against this Philistine to fight with him; for you are just a boy, and he has been a warrior from his youth" (1 Samuel 17:33). But David persisted, and eventually King Saul reluctantly agreed and draped his own armor over David. Unable to walk in Saul's heavy armor, David removed it and appeared on the battlefield dressed in civilian clothing with his hunting sling and five smooth stones.

Goliath appeared disgusted when he saw puny David approaching. He taunted David. David stood resolutely and challenged Goliath:

> You come to me with sword and spear and javelin;
> but I come to you in the name of the Lord of hosts,

the God of the armies of Israel, whom you have
defied. This very day the Lord will deliver you into
my hand . . . and all this assembly may know that
the Lord does not save by sword and spear; for the
battle is the Lord's and he will give you into our
hand (1 Samuel 17:45–47).

With one small stone launched from David's sling, the
impressive Goliath fell

David's triumph is really God's triumph. David is merely
standing in God's place—*the battle is the Lord's*. The message
is this: My God is bigger than this monster. David's courage
comes from his full reliance upon *the Lord*, God. Although this
message may seem to reinforce a religious view of an omnipo-
tent God and weakling human, we can look at the tale from a
metaphysical perspective for a deeper understanding.

Metaphysical interpretation is a deeper look, a personal
look at the characters and details of a story. In metaphysical
interpretation, each character represents an aspect of our own
consciousness.

David, the archetypal hero, represents human innocence
and weakness, unable by itself to courageously meet the challenges of daily living.

The Lord relates to the One Mind or GOD, described
in this book according to many of its recognizable powers.
Remember, all that we can ascribe to GOD, we can claim by
our Divine Identity. The Lord in this story, therefore, can be
understood to be divine strength, the light of stability, courage, and tenacity.

Consider your own David nature that is capable of
standing up to big, scary monsters such as disease, financial

hardships, and other challenges. Despite the voices of Saul, discouraging and self-defeating thoughts, we can rely upon spiritual strength. In the light of spiritual strength, monsters are revealed as illusions. We face them undaunted. As if slaying them with the launch of a small stone, we defeat them by standing stable, courageous, and tenacious. Charles Fillmore taught that spiritual strength always overcomes "the seemingly strong personal and material conditions" (*The Twelve Powers of Man*, 36).

Stability

My husband fell from a ladder and broke his arm in several places. Giles had just begun cleaning the gutters two stories high. He had set the extension ladder in our front garden but it began sinking, so he repositioned it to sit on the sidewalk. As Giles climbed up near the top of the ladder, the base began to slip. I could see it from several feet away but was helpless to stop the ladder, or Giles, from crashing to the ground. Signs of shock. Arm distorted into an unnatural curve. Ambulance. Surgery. Recovery.

A stable base for the ladder would have made for a successful outcome. To be stable is to be rooted in or anchored to a firm foundation. The stabilizing power of strength is our capacity to anchor ourselves securely in the truth of our unlimited source of calm, safety, and balance. We can stand strong during times of change. Strength is our power of stand-ability.

A muscle-bound weightlifter exemplifies strength in the physical body. Standing firmly rooted he is strong, but one wrong move causes him to become unsteady. In addition, those built-up muscles become tight and stiff, which means you'll likely not find a muscle-bound person enjoying a yoga class. The fact is, the stabilizing power of spiritual strength we are after is not only sturdiness but also flexibility.

"The soft and supple are the companions of life, while the stiff and unyielding are the companions of death" (Tao Te Ching, Star, *Two Suns Rising*, 39). The Tao points to a paradoxical truth about the stabilizing power of strength—rigidity is not consistent with this power. Successful application of strength allows for firm resolve in the truth we know, as well as flexibility to respond to situations presenting themselves moment to moment. An example of how this works can be found in an experience most can relate to: job searching. Job searching these days is very different from the era when you introduced yourself personally to prospective employers. Nowadays, job searching primarily takes place online. For many people, job searching this way is frustrating; they imagine their application buried under a mile-long stack that never gets seen. I have visited with many job-seekers, many who have been out of work for long stretches of time and are now feeling anxious, worrying about personal financial collapse and feeling defeated. Such a circumstance is a perfect practice arena for the spiritual power of strength. Imagine you are in this situation. Imagine yourself drawing from your spiritual strength, your stand-ability, standing strong in the insistence of truth.

Truth is: GOD, my Source, is abundance, the principle of plenty. I trust in the abundance of jobs that allow me to give my greatest gifts and receive my greatest good. As I remain anchored in spiritual strength, I unflaggingly commit to being purposeful, clear, optimistic, passionate, and forward-looking in my job search. I refuse to submit to niggling worries and doubts that may arise from time to time. Instead, I do what I know to do, become skilled in job searching, and courageously proceed. Whenever I receive a "no thanks" notice, I remind myself to hold steady, knowing something better is on the horizon. I remember that in an ocean of job possibilities, I need be a match to only one. One job in an ocean of plenty! That's like acquiring one grain of sand on the seashore! I pay attention to signs along the way, internal as well as external, so that I adjust my strategies easily day by day, being responsive to opportunities as they arise. I stay flexible, following hunches and responding to cues that may not appear a perfect fit but could lead me to the something wonderful I am after.

Stable, centered, calm, balanced, rooted, anchored, secure, safe, sturdy yet flexible, strong in character—these are the marks of the stabilizing power of strength.

Courage

Centered in strength, we can proceed boldly. Courage is another aspect of spiritual strength. One of my favorite words, audacity, applies to the power of strength.

In 2003, when I was seeking to be hired by a Unity community as their minister, I was considered to be in a tenuous position. I was in training toward Unity ordination, licensed but not yet ordained. Many colleagues recommended I not set my sights on a full-fledged ministry because a full-size ministry might not be inclined to hire someone of my status. With nothing to lose at this point—I was not at the time serving in a ministry—I sat in prayer activating the power of strength. I concentrated on the stabilizing power until I felt courageous enough to proceed. I became absolutely clear there was a ministry that I would recognize as perfect for my vision, talents, and skills. And they would recognize me. Reminding myself at every turn that I did not need to rely upon anyone's statistics, I became convinced my fate could not be subject to "the way it is" in the world. I swiftly identified five churches that seemed promising to me, and I sent them my paperwork, including a cover letter extolling the value of their hiring a minister-in-training. Audaciously, I expressed that my spiritual community and I would have the benefit of the most contemporary Unity teachings for ministers; that we would have a seasoned mentor supporting us through the process; and other facts that I wholeheartedly believed relevant to any church that would consider me. Instead of attempting to conceal my status, I turned it into an asset.

Two of the five churches immediately dismissed my application because they considered me not qualified. The other three churches interviewed me by telephone and all three invited me for weekend on-site visits. Within three months, considered record time by many Unity ministers, I celebrated my first Sunday at Unity in San Antonio. (June 2013 marked my tenth anniversary.)

My son Adrian was a young teen, soon to lose interest in childhood holiday rituals, when one Halloween he and his friends decided to go trick-or-treating together. Giles and I were surprised when, less than an hour later, Adrian returned home alone. He told us that the rest of his friends thought it would be fun to steal candy from the younger trick-or-treaters. Adrian disagreed. He told them so, and left them on the street.

We all face such dilemmas. We want to go along with the crowd because we want to belong. We want to be liked. We also want to be true, to be in integrity with our values. The courageous power of spiritual strength is valuable when we want to distance ourselves from colleagues telling jokes at the expense of a particular culture, religion, or gender. Strength is valuable when a friend has kept us waiting once again and we have decided to wait no longer. Strength is valuable when we are worried for the safety and well-being of a child in our neighborhood. Strength is valuable when a coworker has taken credit for our innovation. We can practice asserting courage in minor daily matters, fortifying ourselves with strength for greater challenges. Anytime we fail to express courage in a situation, it is never too late. We can always speak to our colleagues later or call our friend the next day.

Bold, inspired, courageous action stemming from spiritual strength makes for a thrilling life experience. It also uplifts one and all.

Tenacity

In 1953, a year before I was born, a start-up company experimented with a rust-prevention solvent for the aerospace industry. One attempt after another failed. Twenty times. Thirty times. Thirty-nine times. On the fortieth try, WD-40 was created. WD-40 stands for "water-displacement perfected on the fortieth try." Today, a can of WD-40 sits on a shelf in my house, and houses all across the globe (www.wd40.com), evidence of a tenacious team.

Tenacity, also labeled perseverance, persistence, and stamina, is a useful component of the power of strength.

Tenacity provides us staying power. Drawing forth tenacity during unsteady circumstances means not giving up prematurely and remaining committed in our stand-ability, persistently acting with confidence.

One morning on retreat, while silently sipping coffee outdoors, I listened to life going on around me. The Cibolo Creek was babbling. A red bird called from a nearby tree, two high-pitched whistles followed by seven chirps, over and over again. Shrubbery rustled in a light breeze. The day had begun. Swiping at my leg in response to feeling something on it, I saw the "something" was not a dried oak leaf like the ones that were raining all over me. I swiped at a small caterpillar-like critter. It landed on the deck next to my chair. Being in a state of quiet awareness, I watched the insect place some feet in front of the others as it inched along. It moved, undaunted, over the gaps between deck slats. It found the leg of my chair and began climbing. When it reached the top, it projected more than half its mass over the edge of the chair, feeling for its next support and finding it on the surface of the table close by. It kept going until it could not sense a surface on which to proceed, at which time it doubled back, curled its long body around, arcing like a divining rod until it found solid land. All the other feet followed.

The busy little creature traveled a great distance, by caterpillar standards. It never seemed to be concerned with whether it was upright or sideways, retracing its steps or in new territory. Every time it came to an abyss, it paused long enough to feel its way to the next solid ground.

I was thinking, as I observed the creature teacher, that I would do well to feel my way forward by the power of tenacity.

Persisting non-anxiously is the activity of tenacity. Tenacity, along with stability and courage, makes up the habits of spiritual strength.

Meditation for Strength

To connect with the power of strength in my body, I begin by standing. I stand tall, with my feet positioned shoulder width apart. I lift my shoulders, press them back, and drop them down. I tuck my chin slightly, pressing the crown of my head up as if to hold up the ceiling. I breathe in. Hold. Breathe out. Hold the posture while softening my stance. A few more times I breathe in. Hold. Breathe out.

I center attention on the small of my back, the center of the spiritual power of strength. Here converge strong bones, flexible ligaments and tendons, large muscles and highly sensitive nerves. The small of the back is designed to be incredibly strong, protecting delicate nerve roots, yet highly flexible, providing for mobility.

I shine the light of verdant spring green through the area where my back curves at the waistline. I shine light throughout the abdominal cavity, out to embrace my body, out beyond my body, spreading across the earth like the invisible kingdom of the heavens.

Sitting, I repeat the words "I AM divine strength" or "I AM spiritual strength." I concentrate on this truth idea. Gradually, I go deeper into silence, the wordless state of deep meditation.

When ready, I affirm: Divine strength is my spiritual name and nature. I AM strong, stable, and steadfast in body, mind, and spirit. I AM the power of stand-ability, anchored to the shore while the winds of change swirl around me. I am centered in truth during times of instability. I am rooted to GOD, my source of strength. By spiritual strength, I am confident, courageous, and determined, faithful to the truth I know. I am responsive from my position of spiritual strength. I claim these divine attributes, trusting they are part of the intelligence within the very cells of my body and throughout every dimension of my being. I appreciate my limitless power to stay strong in all circumstances. I AM spiritual strength, stable, courageous, and tenacious.

Practices to Cultivate Strength

1. Read the Meditation for Strength daily, or make an audio recording and listen to it daily. Choose one of the affirmations in the meditation to recite and contemplate.

2. Write about strength in your journal. Here are some questions you might choose to reflect upon:

   • What do you rely upon as your foundation, that which stabilizes you?

   • Thinking about your current hopes and dreams, what role could courage play? If you were courageous, what might you do?

   • Remember the details of times in your life when you were tenacious.

   • Identify a situation in your present experience that calls for the light of strength. What thoughts and acts could demonstrate stability, courage, and tenacity?

3. Create or select a symbol for strength to display where you will see it often. Here are some examples: an image of or actual tree branch; an original drawing, collage, or sculpture.

4. Practice the upright posture described in the first paragraph of the Meditation for Strength. From an upright position, bend at the waist into a forward bend. Linger in the forward bend while concentrating on the small of your back. Sense the seat of strength in your body.

10

THE LIGHT OF ORDER—
THE POWER OF ORGANIZATION,
ADJUSTMENT, AND EVOLUTION

For everything there is a season, and a time for every matter under heaven: a time to be born, and a time to die; a time to plant, and a time to pluck up what is planted.

—Ecclesiastes 3:1-2

Order is the first law of the universe. Indeed there could be no universe unless its various parts were kept in perfect harmony.

—Charles Fillmore, *Mysteries of Genesis*

ONE NIGHT AWAY FROM THE city, viewing the night sky unobstructed by clouds, I giddily identified the Big Dipper, the Little Dipper, and Venus as I had done years before at summer camp. I thought about the constancy of these images throughout history. My eyes were fixed on heavenly bodies recognizable in the sky that Jesus of Nazareth viewed, and before him, Gautama Buddha. They are reliable markers of planet Earth's location in space.

The sun rises and sets. Winter gives way to spring. Apple seeds grow into apple trees. Human birth occurs in the ninth month after conception. One plus one equals two.

Order is built into all of life. Order is the architecture of the universe. Everything, from the spirals of a nautilus to a hexagonal honeycomb, from infinity lines to ever-expanding circles, displays an orderliness that dazzles scientists and theologians alike.

Order fascinates us. We rely upon it. We study and make meaning of it. For example, every ancient culture, no matter how isolated, incorporated spirals into their recordkeeping. Spirals represented creation, growth, and development, invisible yet sensed order, immortality, and the circle of life. The spiral is a popular image in modern culture. The *koru* (a Māori word meaning "loop" or "spiral"), often used in Māori art as a symbol of creation, is based on the shape of an unfurling fern frond. The koru represents new life. It is the symbol of beginnings, the undeveloped potential awaiting its fulfillment. It is also the symbol for renewal, bringing to mind the cycle of seasons and new growth in springtime. The koru symbolizes transformation, or moving from one state of being into another. Its spiral shape conveys the idea of perpetual movement, signifying continuous growth and vitality. Like a new fern shoot arising from the ground to reach toward the light, the koru represents our reach toward enlightenment or realization of oneness.

The order we sense and experience in the natural world is a material representation of spiritual order, the intelligent underlying and overarching, though invisible, order out of which all becomes possible. When the material world—and our circumstances—appear random rather than orderly, we doubt the reality of spiritual order. The world seems particularly out of order when a child dies before her parents, when an armed assailant opens fire during a public celebration, when a limb must be severed to spare the rest of the body, or when a lover leaves inexplicably. Either the universe is unfair, we may think, or God knows what we do not know.

"God's will" is often the explanation for inexplicable circumstances. It must be God's will! When we do not like what is happening or where we are in relationship to where we would rather be, it must be God's will! The failure of human reasoning to comprehend divine order has led to superstition and anthropomorphizing GOD: God wanted that child in heaven; God allows humans to suffer on earth so they will be happy in the afterlife; God wants our misery so we will turn to him. But wait! GOD is not a superhuman personality that imposes order. Rather, GOD *is* order, the organizing principle revealed in the pattern and sequence inherent in all of life. Divine order is not a correction of some unhappy condition but an integrated arrangement of energy in a pattern, sequence, or method.

When my sister Maureen died by suicide thirteen years ago, my family and I suffered unspeakable sorrow. In common with others whose loved ones take their own lives, I grieved guiltily, thinking I should have noticed forewarning signs or stayed in closer contact with my sister. I searched my soul and sought spiritual support in an effort to make sense of this seemingly senseless circumstance.

I felt guilty for having distanced myself from Maureen during the year and a half preceding her death. Our relationship had become one-sided as Maureen withdrew from most human contact during that time. I stopped telephoning her as regularly as I had in earlier years, because it was painful to hear Maureen's voice reduced to a whisper and her interest in life waning. A minister accustomed to praying with people and lifting their spirits, I felt helpless and useless with Maureen, who would not allow mention of healing or spirituality. I had done all I could do, all Maureen would permit, so I withdrew in resignation. I regretted, afterward, that I had withdrawn due to my own frustration without considering the message my sister might have received by my telephone calls: that I loved her and cared about her well-being.

I regretted that my sister died alone, in pain. I had sorrowfully observed Maureen's deteriorating mental health over many years. I held no religious or moral objection to Maureen's insistence on self-determination. Therefore, had Maureen told me of her suicide plan, I believe I would have held her hand through it.

Guilt and regret made my grief complicated. I will always remember the moment I released guilt and regret, when I could feel "clean" grief. It happened during a session of spiritual counseling, when I challenged myself to discern the underlying and overarching order inherent in all circumstances. Glimpsing eternity, I recategorized Maureen's death as a benign occurrence that made perfect sense in light of Maureen's desire for relief from a punishing, malfunctioning human brain. Shifting my attention from my personal experience to a universal view, I relinquished guilt as I realized that Maureen's mind in eternity could not harbor blame, could not fathom any only-human sense of separation. I had been operating from a myopic, limited awareness, but now I could simply feel sad for my loss of my sister's physical presence. In time, my sadness too dissipated as I encountered Maureen in my memories and, occasionally, in a random acerbic thought I recognized as a Maureen-ism.

When a hawk stalks, kills, and eats a dove, most people recognize this violence as consistent with natural order. Were we to suspend human moralism and religiosity regarding the many challenging and disturbing occurrences in our own lives, we might more easily access the inherent order that *is* in every moment, in all dimensions.

When my loved one dies, when I get laid off from my job, when I run out of money and my car gets repossessed, when my lover leaves . . . naturally, humanly, I grieve. Also, I assert my rightful power of order. I claim the power of spiritual organization, adjustment, and evolution.

Organization

In the northeast region of the United States, where I lived during childhood, a first mark of springtime was the blossoming of my backyard forsythia bush. When it burst into bright yellow blooms, I could be absolutely certain that the forsythia bush in my girlfriend's yard had also flowered. All the forsythias in the region, on an indiscernible cue, sprang to life. Today, I live in south Texas, where we mark spring by the bloom of bluebonnets. When one bluebonnet plant blooms, we can presume that in optimal conditions of light, moisture, and temperature all other bluebonnets will be blooming as well.

Order is the framework, structure, pattern, and sequence at the heart of all that lives. The organizing principle of order is evident in all of nature: "The earth produces of itself, first the stalk, then the head, then the full grain in the head" (Mark 4:28). Order underlies music and mathematics. Search online for "the beauty of math" and you will find stunning images of mathematical order.

Observing the organizing principle in the manifest world, we obtain clues about how to create our own experience. We wield our spiritual power of order in this sequence: mind, idea, and manifestation. Mind, or Divine Mind, is the essential oneness often referred to as GOD, or Spirit, universal intelligence, or the kingdom of the heavens. Mind is the source of all possibilities, all that can be. One with mind, we have access to all that can be. We catch hold of one idea in the One Mind, and we develop that one idea by use of our spiritual abilities, such as imagination, faith, wisdom, etc. The idea dwells in us. It grows as a seed grows in fertile soil. We water it with enthusiasm and anticipation. The idea manifests as our experience.

Several years before I met my friend Connie, her sixteen-year-old daughter died from injuries sustained in a car accident. I was surprised at how "okay" Connie seemed, as I could not conceive of how a mother could go on living after her child's death. I learned that Connie did not get to "okay" all at once. For a long while, her terrible grief seemed interminable. Connie had a firm foundation in spiritual understanding, however, which convinced her that her daughter was not dead in an eternal sense; that everlasting life was a reality; and that her daughter was and always would be with her. Connie was tuned to Divine Mind, the ultimate truth beyond all appearances. Out of this understanding came the idea Connie was seeking: that all was well with her daughter and that she, Connie, could live in peace. Connie worked with this idea over time, feeling reassured over and over again in moments of connection with her daughter that urged her toward acceptance. Connie dipped her toes into the current of her life streaming toward the future, knowing it would be all right, and not a betrayal, for her to be happy. I am unable to describe Connie's knowing in human language because she *felt* rather than thought this idea. When Connie speaks of her daughter these days, her smile fills her face with light.

In a state of oneness consciousness, Connie caught the divine idea of uninterruptible, incorruptible divine life. She caught the divine idea of unifying, harmonizing divine love. She held these ideas in mind, as truths to be realized, until they became her lived reality.

Each of us, by nature, is capable of tuning to the intelligent order that is the framework, structure, pattern, and sequence at the heart of all that can ever be. We are capable of organizing our thoughts, words, and actions in concert with divine order: "Even in the small details of life, such as dress, conversation, eating, sleeping, and working, system and order enable one to live a richer and fuller life" (Fillmore, *Mysteries of Genesis*, 241).

Adjustment

Adjustment is a feature of order. Adjustment in the body occurs through homeostasis, the body's effort to regulate optimum conditions for health. Similarly, the natural world is continually adjusting to changing conditions and reestablishing order. What appears to be a catastrophic natural disaster, such as a forest fire not caused by human action, is nature's way of adjusting conditions in the interest of long-range health of the planet.

Spiritually, adjustment is our power of modifying thoughts, words, and actions to support our wholeness of being. We flip a switch or shift our awareness to adapt to new spiritual understanding or to modify our habits of thought and feeling. Spiritual practices such as meditating, journaling, releasing, and saying affirmations provide a process—an order—for conditioning, or adjusting, our consciousness.

Perhaps you can relate to this perpetual balancing act: I benefit from being busy. I thoroughly enjoy filling my calendar with meaningful, interesting activities. I also benefit from being still. I relish times of meditation as well as physical, mental, and spiritual rest.

Action and stillness may appear to be opposites, but rather than opposing each other, they support each other. Action and stillness are examples not of polar opposites but of polarities. Barry Johnson, PhD, author of *Polarity Management*, teaches that polarities are not problems; they are equal values that we all juggle, unavoidable energies that we all deal with, within ourselves. Whenever we reflect, "I need more balance in my life," we are unknowingly acknowledging our desire to adjust one or more polarities.

Action and stillness in my experience are like summer and winter, two distinct seasons. Among the disciplines of yoga practice, action is akin to Karma Yoga and stillness is akin to Rāja Yoga. Life would be incomplete without both of them; they each fulfill an important purpose; and one well observed enriches the other.

> Jesus said, "If they say to you, 'Where have you come from?' say to them, 'We have come from the light, from the place where the light came into being by itself, established {itself}, and appeared in their image.' If they say to you, 'Is it you?' say, 'We are its children, and we are the chosen of the living Father.' If they ask you, 'What is the evidence of your Father in you?' say to them, 'It is motion and rest'" (Thomas 50).

Motion and rest, action and stillness, are coequal spiritual values. One is as important as the other for the fullness of life. When I am active, my body thrives and my brain is engaged in creativity. I feel productive. I enjoy the stimulation of preparing and executing a plan. I relish the feeling of satisfaction at the end of a busy day. Filling my calendar with appointments for work and play gives me joy, for I recognize the pleasure I derive from every chosen activity.

Keeping busy, I can go a long while before I begin to feel run-down. At some point, I will look at all the hours I have scheduled and realize I feel stretched too thin, overscheduled. All that I had been eagerly anticipating now feels like a demand. Pleasurable activities such as gardening now have to be squeezed in, which turns them into jobs that need to be done. I am so busy that I skip morning meditation, journaling, yoga, and other mind-quieting practices. I have no time for dreaming or meaning making. I begin to suffer agitation, anxiousness, and spiritual aridity. Sufficiently provoked by discomfort, I realize I am starved for stillness.

When I am still, I retreat from the world and other people into a cocoon of peace. My mind quiets. I return to my source of being, universal oneness during extended meditation. I am at home within myself. I am centered spiritually, renewed. I live in the moment, being rather than doing. Deeply, I rest.

If I remain on retreat too long, I begin to feel mentally dull and unfocused. Lack of interaction with others can result in self-delusion and a sense of disconnection. A need for structure and activity arises as a feeling of restlessness. These stirrings propel me into action by the adjusting power of order.

Previous generations of self-help education emphasized balance, which meant a kind of mental and emotional homeostasis. The idea was that if we could somehow achieve an ideal balance of activity and stillness, and hold there, life would be smooth sailing from that point forward. The quest to achieve a once-and-for-all balance left most people feeling inadequate when they could not maintain such a balance day to day. How many times in your life have you achieved what seems a perfect balance in your morning routine: You awaken early to meditate, work out at the gym, get yourself—as well as the children and the pets—ready for the day. You are balancing stillness and activity, home and work, taking care of your kids and teaching them to be independent . . . One morning, you feel ill. Or your child feels ill. Or it's a holiday and everyone sleeps in. Or you go on vacation. It doesn't take much to interrupt the delicate balance we all seem to strive for, as if that perfect schedule could extend into eternity. It cannot.

It is impossible to remain perpetually balanced. Our daily schedules are not like a balancing act. They are more like a juggling act. Only one juggling pin at a time can be held in the hand. Likewise, only one item can be attended to at any time. The adjusting power of order is our ability to shift our attention to the other polarity. Our adjusting ability is inherent. It is born of wisdom—our power of judgment, discernment, and intuition—and, like juggling, it is a simple matter of opening our mind to sense the weight and shape of the pin we are catching. By the power of order, and by our focused intention, we know what we need moment by moment, whether it is activity or stillness, structure or flexibility, tradition or innovation, independence or dependence upon others: "The divine idea of order is the idea of adjustment, and as this is established in a person's thought, his or her mind and affairs will be at one with the universal harmony" (Fillmore, *The Revealing Word*, 143). Our ability to adjust is a rich spiritual resource from which we draw to bolster an affirmative outlook on life. Activating our power to adjust, we literally change our energy, shift our awareness, uplift our attitude, and transform our life.

Evolution

I used to feel envious of people who devoted all their working years to a single career. When I was a practicing massage therapist, one of my several careers, a client was retiring from a job he had held for thirty-five years. I was in awe of his accomplishment. My father and mother were also faithful to their work; Dad was an electrical contractor and Mom was a full-time homemaker. I was not cut from their cloth. I possessed a seemingly inborn restlessness. I changed jobs every few years, and I worried about myself every time I got the itch that led to a switch. I thought something was wrong with me. Why couldn't I settle somewhere and be happy like most other people seemed to do?

I was loving my work as a massage therapist. Every person left feeling better than when they had arrived. I served one person at a time, established a thriving full-time practice with faithful clientele, built a beautiful office in my home, had time between clients and after hours for my family and home projects, and was enrolled in Unity's spiritual education. I was my own boss. I was in the midst of a high time in my life. Soon, though, I felt a resurgence of restlessness. I could not ignore it this time because the thought that impressed itself in my mind was that it was time to play in a larger arena. The good that I was doing one person at a time I could be doing by spreading the Unity message as a teacher or—really?—a minister! Days, weeks, and months went by as I did my best to ignore this inner urge that I had not asked for. I loved my work!

My divine discontent continued, and before long the minister at my local Unity church approached me about joining his staff. I reduced my massage therapy load to half-time and served Unity of Omaha half-time as the associate pastor. It all made sense. I was evolving.

Evolution is the power of order demonstrated as development, progress, or growth. In spiritual circles, evolution is often referred to as spiritual unfolding or transformation. Evolution moves in the direction of expansion, from simple to complex. Our ability to evolve is inherent, just as evolution is inherent in the universe. The idea of evolution or harmonious expansion is a divine idea flowing from the Source or One Mind. Our urge to evolve comes from our catching that divine idea and cooperating with it. Charles Fillmore taught, "Involution always precedes evolution. That which is involved in mind evolves through matter" (*The Twelve Powers of Man*, 54).

The idea I had caught of ministering to a larger population I could have ignored. I could have, but I felt the idea as a physical stimulus. I sensed the idea as a compelling possibility. The idea "involved" me—and before long, I could not separate the idea from my identity. From the One Mind to my human mind, from my human mind to my being—this is the power of evolution. Fillmore said it this way:

> Evolution is the result of the development of ideas in mind. What we are is the result of the evolution of our consciousness, and our consciousness is the result of the seed ideas sown in our mind. Therefore spiritual evolution is the unfolding of the Spirit of God into expression. It is the development achieved by {individuals} working under spiritual law (*Keep a True Lent*, 165).

Meditation for Order

Assuming a familiar posture supportive of meditation, I focus my attention on the splendid order in my body temple. Bone, muscle, skin, vortexes of nerves and energy, all organized for physical vitality and strength. Breath flowing in and out, effortlessly. Heart beating rhythmically, steadily, faithfully. I celebrate divine order.

Concentrating my attention within my body, behind my navel, I activate my body's center for order. I shine the verdant green light of order around my digestive organs and throughout the integrated, linked, and well-ordered systems in my body.

Order is my name and my nature. I AM the power of order, by which I connect with my innate sense of direction. I naturally attune to the magnificent Source, the One Mind from which all ideas flow. I catch divine ideas and bring them into manifestation by the power of order.

I AM the adjusting power of order, easily sensing where to place my attention, adjust my mindset, or correct my course of action.

I AM the evolving power of order, awakened to my ever-unfolding consciousness. I incorporate the best of my past into my present and reach, naturally, toward a fuller and more enlightened future.

By the power of order, I follow the clear path. I go through the open door. I choose an orderly course of thought and action. I bring about order moment by moment, choice by choice.

Practices to Cultivate Order

1. Read the Meditation for Order daily, or make an audio recording and listen to it daily. Choose one of the affirmations in the meditation to recite and contemplate.

2. Write about order in your journal. Here are some questions you might choose to reflect upon:

   - Collect a keepsake from nature the next time you enjoy the outdoors. Contemplate its perfection, beauty, and order. What does this object signify about the power of order? What wisdom does this object reveal to you about your own capacity for order?

- Describe how life works for you when you feel organized. How does organization in your environment impact your state of being?

- Write about a set of polarities you experience, such as work and play, structure and flexibility, or tradition and innovation. Describe the benefits of each of these coequal values. Identify the symptoms you experience when you are over-relying on one and needing to turn your attention to the other.

- Trace your evolution in one area of your life: for example, romantic relationships, parenting, career path, or spirituality. Recognize where your understanding has expanded and your skills have matured.

3. Create or select a symbol for order to display where you will see it often. Here are some examples: an abacus or calculator; a packet of flower or vegetable seeds; an original drawing, collage, or sculpture.

4. Learn a new dance or exercise routine, observing how you internalize the instruction and follow a pattern.

11

THE LIGHT OF RELEASE—
THE POWER OF CLEANSING,
RENUNCIATION, AND REPENTANCE

Every plant that my heavenly Father has not planted will be uprooted.

—Matthew 15:13

There must be a renunciation or letting go of old thoughts before the new can find place in the consciousness. This is a psychological law, which has its outer expression in the intricate eliminative functions of the body.

—Charles Fillmore, *The Twelve Powers of Man*

JESUS WAS HUNGRY. WALKING PAST a fig tree that had no fruit, Jesus cursed the fig tree. Surely Jesus knew that no fig tree in the region would contain fruit at the time, because it was not the season for figs. But Jesus was hungry. He cursed the fig tree. The next day when passing the tree again, his disciples noticed the tree had withered (Mark 11:12–14; 20).

In my early twenties, I was living alone in an apartment. A young man I knew stopped by to take me for a ride in his new car. We ended up at the apartment he shared with his girlfriend, who was not at home. At knifepoint, he intended to rape me. I did everything I could think of to stall him until, miraculously, his girlfriend arrived home unexpectedly and I escaped. A few years later I had an opportunity to heal from this horror when in an intensive energy and Gestalt therapy experience I began shaking and screaming, yelling from my gut at full voice: "You can hurt my body, but you can't hurt ME!" Over and over, I asserted the truth of the Infinite Self.

In the past, I felt uncomfortable reading the fig tree account in the Gospels. I thought it revealed a distasteful side of Jesus. I couldn't get past how Jesus killed a perfectly innocent and useful tree. Rethinking the story by metaphysical interpretation, however, I saw that Jesus was demonstrating how to effectively utilize the spiritual tool named *denial* or *release.* He renounced all that was nonproductive. That's what I did, what my Infinite Self knew to do, when I felt wounded. I renounced the nonproductive idea that any human condition could interfere with my divine nature.

Healing results from aptly applying the divine power of release or elimination. Erase the false. Return to the true—our immutable, irrepressible Divine Identity.

Spiritual release is our power to cleanse, renounce, and repent.

Congestion of some kind is the most reliable symptom prompting us to assert the power of release. In the body, congestion may manifest as constipation or arteriosclerosis. As in the body, so in the mind. Charles Fillmore taught: "The mind, like the bowels, should be open and free" (*The Twelve Powers of Mind*, 144).

Life flows, naturally. Always, life is streaming. Bodies of water flow through inlets and outlets. A body of water stopped either at its inlet or outlet stagnates. It stinks. It dies. Damming the mind with unforgiveness, self-criticism, or nonconstructive beliefs produces stinking thinking. Utilize any of these three aspects of the purgative power of release and you will not only feel better but you will know more surely your Infinite Self, your Divine Identity.

Cleansing

The ritual of baptism in Christian communities stems from John the Baptizer in the Bible, who was Jesus' ascetic cousin. John wore "clothing of camel's hair with a leather belt around his waist, and his food was locusts and wild honey" (Matthew 3:4). He baptized people in the Jordan River, cleansing their sins to "prepare the way of the Lord" (Matthew 3:3). Ever since, I believe, most of us have grossly misunderstood the beauty of—and the practicality of—the cleansing power of release.

Bathing or showering is meant to refresh by gently removing or dissolving dirt and dead skin. I have memories from childhood of scrubbing my skin so briskly, and with such harsh soaps, that my skin became raw and sore—not exactly the intention of cleansing. My parents didn't know, and I didn't know back then, that gentle action is all that is needed.

I've never cured constipation by force, either; or improved my financial position by stockpiling every dollar that came my way; or erased a bad memory by retelling the sad story to anyone who would listen. The cleansing action of release is meant to be gentle, allowing rather than forcing. It is meant to clear the body and mind, restoring equanimity. Think in terms of melting ice, softening muscles, or easing strain.

Mentally, sins as addressed by John the Baptizer can be thought of as *dirt*. Sins are mistakes we have made, lies we have told, facts we have withheld, confidences we have broken, and all manner of integrity breaches. Sins are our misperceptions and misunderstandings of divine nature and our Divine Identity. Dirt/sin on the skin of our Infinite Self can be removed or dissolved with a gentle shower of awareness. Dirt/sin does not penetrate, but is a veneer on the surface that does not damage the underlying substance. Sin, contrary to centuries of thought, is not and cannot be an offense against God or a deliberate turning away from God, causing our estrangement from God. Nothing can separate us from GOD, the divine nature that is our most true, Infinite Self. Only in our mind can we feel separate; and when we feel separate, we can cleanse our mind with the power of release.

Cleansing leads to refreshment. The refresh button on a computer restores the web page or document desired. The cleansing action of release restores our awareness of our original and true divine nature.

Renunciation

John the Baptizer renounced the comforts of conventional living. He released identification with his finite self—aka ego or only-human consciousness—in favor of his Infinite Self or Divine Identity. John's attempts at erasing only-human consciousness were severe, stemming from condemnation of his human nature. Charles Fillmore reflected that John's severity in self-denial led to his condemning Herod, for which he lost his head: "The ascetic takes the route of denial so energetically that he starves his powers instead of transforming them" (*The Twelve Powers of Man*, 152). Beware, therefore, that our renunciation is of our sense of limitation rather than of our humanity. Releasing only-human consciousness is releasing our sense of limitation. When we release our belief that "I am only human," we uncover our Divine Identity that has been intact all along. We do not have to acquire our Divine Identity; we only need release a limited sense of self, our finite self, to reveal the Infinite Self.

A familiar symbol in most Christian communities is the cross or crucifix, representing Jesus' death by crucifixion, understood conventionally as Jesus' act of salvation for all humanity. There is another way to understand the cross, one that is not tied to any denominational dogma. The cross is a fitting symbol for our release ability. By his crucifixion and death, Jesus demonstrated release of any sense of himself as limited. He overcame the limitation of death. He released all ties to only-human awareness so that his Infinite Self arose supreme.

In the activity of spiritual release, we *cross out* in consciousness our only-human sense of self so that the true Self, our Divine Identity, rises into prominence in all we think, say, and do. Fillmore taught, "Every time we give up error there is a crucifixion" (*Keep a True Lent*, 195).

True for all our spiritual abilities, the renouncing aspect of release operates on the physical, mental, and spiritual levels of consciousness. Recently, Alan Chambers, the former president of Exodus International, the largest Christian organization in the world, stunningly closed operations on a forty-year effort to heal homosexuality as if it were a disease. He reached conclusions over time that countered his premise that you could pray the gay away, promising to make amends to thousands who have been harmed by Exodus's methods.

Mental application of renunciation is far more challenging than closing the doors of a business. Fillmore taught:

> The beliefs that you and your ancestors have held in mind have become thought currents so strong that their course in you can be changed only by your resolute decision to entertain them no longer. They will not be turned out unless the ego through whose domain they run decides positively to adopt means of casting them out of his consciousness, and at the same time erects gates that will prevent their inflow from external sources. This is done by denial and affirmation; the denial always comes first (*The Twelve Powers of Man*, 154).

Thought crystallization is the mental counterpart to saline buildup in the Dead Sea that has an inlet but no outlet. Salt is a preservative, crystallizing history, so to speak. Thought crystallizes around a long-held belief that gets reinforced in our experience. For example, a woman heard repeatedly through childhood the idea, "you'll never get anywhere in life unless you work hard." Now an adult, she works hard and feels disdain for people who play at their work. She takes life seriously, is dutiful and perfectionistic, and wishes she could lighten up. The truism has crystallized into a solid belief pattern that has sucked joy from her life. Although this is an extreme example, and simplistic, it illustrates the challenge of releasing mental constructs. Learning and rigorously practicing denial, or release, followed by affirmation can be a long-term approach to removing the power of long-standing beliefs. More detail about denials and affirmations is available in chapter 4 of my 2011 book, *How to Pray Without Talking to God*.

Spiritually, renunciation takes place when we cultivate an open mind and open heart, giving up every thought and belief we have clung to, becoming teachable through the activity of spiritual understanding.

Repentance

The related Judeo-Christian terms *salvation*, *conversion*, and *sanctification* factor into the power of release. Salvation, or redemption, is understood traditionally to come from a God outside ourselves, or from God through Jesus Christ's sacrifice, to a spiritually impoverished—sinful—humanity. Conversion is an awakening from the darkness of ignorance about God to the light of spiritual awareness. Sanctification is making holy that which has been profane.

As we have come to know that GOD is not an actor from afar, and that GOD is not a superhuman who would demand and direct a bloody sacrifice of his own son, we have needed to reinterpret salvation and related terms.

Jesus was a teacher. He taught through his living and his dying. He spoke words and demonstrated through actions a way of being driven by inner wisdom. That he named this wisdom *Father* tells us that wisdom is related to us; it is our

Source. Jesus taught principles, or laws, that we may follow as he did to achieve what he did:

> We have thought that we were to be saved by Jesus making personal petitions and sacrifices for us, but now we see that we are to be saved by using the creative principles that he developed in himself . . . (Charles Fillmore, *Jesus Christ Heals*, 162).

> Our salvation is in our living by the Christ pattern—not only by the teachings of the man Jesus Christ but by the Christ Mind within us (Myrtle Fillmore, *How to Let God Help You*, 53).

We work out our own salvation by changing our mind. We convert, and we awaken to our sacredness by studying, meditating on, and adopting the living principles as taught by Jesus and other masters the world over. Our salvation, conversion, or sanctification is preceded by a release of beliefs and ways of being that no longer make sense to us in light of our growing new understanding. We repent.

As a Roman Catholic child, my repentance for swearing or disobeying my parents was to recite the Hail Mary a certain number of times. It seemed to me these were incantations meant to magically restore me to God's favor. I was forgiven, and yet I knew I would swear again and disobey again. There is an unsavory side to repentance in religious history, as well: the severe self-punishment of ascetics intent upon battering their body to get the devil out of their mind. Why? So they could be worthy of God's love.

Let's demystify the idea of repentance. The Greek word *metanoeo*, translated into English as "repent," means a change in mind/consciousness. Although it means, secondarily, to abhor one's past sins, metanoeo contains no hint of any need for punishment. The Hebrew word *shuwb*, also translated into English as "repent," means "to return, restore, come back, or turn back." No condemnation implied. No self-flagellation required; only a releasing of the past.

Repentance and forgiveness work together in Judeo-Christian theology. The premise is that God forgives us when we are truly repentant. When we understand that to repent is to change our mind, to return to our awareness of our true nature, what is there to forgive? Returning to our Divine Identity or Infinite Self, we have restored our awareness of oneness. We have revivified body, mind, and spirit.

Meditation for Release

I concentrate attention at the lowest point on my spine, the site of a cluster of nerve cells directing elimination of bodily waste. I shine earth-tone light throughout my lower pelvis containing organs of elimination. Expanding the reach of the light, I radiate light into my abdominal cavity containing digestive organs, liver, and kidneys, and into my lungs. I expand to the borders of my body, where my skin is the largest organ of elimination.

I bless and appreciate my body's natural capacity to release chemicals that would harm my health if accumulated and never eliminated. I bless and appreciate my mental capacity to release the past, to drop unhealthy patterns of behavior, to forgive, and to free myself from untrue assumptions and beliefs that disempower me. I celebrate my spiritual release ability.

I am not merely a physical body. I am not an only-human. I am not limited by my age, ethnicity, education, or any human factor. I cannot be weak or unworthy. I release my best human understanding about myself, GOD, others, and life itself so that I am open to new insights. I release past judgments and condemnations of myself and others. I cleanse from my mind ridiculous ideas of lack and limitation.

Release is my spiritual name and nature. I naturally and effortlessly release wasteful thoughts of unworthiness and only-human limitation. With every breath, I release the moment past, that I might be wholeheartedly present now.

Practices to Cultivate Release

1. Read the Meditation for Release daily, or make an audio recording and listen to it daily. Choose one of the affirmations in the meditation to recite and contemplate.

2. Write about release in your journal. Here are some questions you might choose to reflect upon:

   - At bedtime, list all the things from your day that you are willing to release. Include attitudes, such as resentment or possessiveness; untrue beliefs, such as unworthiness or sinfulness; memories, good and bad; and states of mind, such as perfectionism or resistance. Commit to this practice of release for at least a week.

   - Recognize a long-standing belief that seems to limit you or cause a negative stream of thought. For example, *I can't afford it*. Examine the roots of this belief. Identify the earliest memory you have of hearing it or internalizing it. Name some unwanted effects of this belief. Imagine treating this belief with the cleansing action of release. What could happen if you were to renounce this belief?

- Reflect upon an unhappy occurrence from your past that when you think about it now continues to stimulate painful or negative thoughts and feelings. Considering the power of repentance, what could be your next act toward changing your mind, forgiving yourself as well as others, and laying this situation to rest?

- Contemplate the ultimate release, which is death. If you were close with a loved one who has died, what did his or her experience teach you about the power of release? What stages or degrees of release have you experienced as you've grieved? If you have given thought to your own death, what do you imagine would be most difficult to release, and why? What would you consider a "good" death?

3. Create or select a symbol for release to display where you will see it often. Here are some examples: an eraser; a small bowl of water; an original drawing, collage, or sculpture.

4. Clean out the garage, give away unused clothing, donate some of your money to a worthwhile cause, or choose another tangible act of release. Afterward, appreciate the effects of cleared space.

~~~

12

~~~

THE LIGHT OF LIFE—
THE POWER OF ANIMATION,
VITALITY, AND PRESENCE

*Then the Lord God formed man from the dust of the ground,
and breathed into his nostrils the breath of life; and the man
became a living being.*

—Genesis 2:7

*The first step in the realization of life is always to know that
God is life, abundant, omnipresent, eternal, and this second step
is to make positive connection with God life by declaring oneness
with it.*

—Charles Fillmore, *Keep a True Lent*

CHILDREN LIKE DISASSEMBLING TOYS TO see what's inside. Curious minds endeavor to know the mechanisms at work behind the scenes. Humans have always and probably always will strive to see smaller and smaller building blocks of life as well as larger and larger spans of space.

We have reduced biological structures to their smallest parts until we could break them down no further and discovered, to the surprise of everyone, that invisible space itself is alive.

Current astronomical research has revealed that it's not your father's galaxy. In the sixties we knew of nine planets, including the humble Pluto that was "new" in 1930 but today has been downgraded and kicked out of the planetary kingdom. The world, however, is not shrinking. "Astronomers announced there are at least 100 billion planets in our Milky Way Galaxy alone, many of them rocky and Earth-size." Another astronomer says these planets are so common that our galaxy must be "swarming with little habitable planets . . ." (Eric Berger, *Houston Chronicle*, January 11, 2012).

Let's face it, there is more and ever more to learn about life. Isn't this the meaning of "abundant life," that we might find ever-increasing knowledge of life itself, with ever-expanding possibilities for expressing that life and ever-unfolding worlds—manifestations—of it?

Life is of divine origin. Life is eternal and indestructible, in keeping with the first law of thermodynamics: Energy cannot be created or destroyed. Although invisible and nonmaterial, evidence of life can be sensed. Life exists in potential and requires intentionality, direction. Life is not a creation of the body; the body cannot create or destroy life. Life gives rise to the body. Invisible life takes shape in visible forms.

Life as a principle and spiritual ability is not to be confused with *human* life. A human life—specifically, a human body—has a beginning and an end in our time-space reality. A human body is said to "live" between a birth and a death. Life, the principle and spiritual ability, has no such finite existence. Life is eternal, which means it has always been, is now, and always shall be.

All that has form in materiality, including a human body, can be threatened or compromised, depleted or exhausted, whereas life the principle and power is indestructible. Life cannot be diminished. Life continually renews.

The principle of life, our life faculty, expresses as animation, vitality, and presence.

Animation

The animating power of life is its forward, onward, and upward impulse. Life is in constant motion, ever expansive in the macro and the micro, in gross as well as subtle expressions. The animating power of life is the evolutionary force.

Natural life is not of itself intelligent. The animating force unguided by wisdom, faith, or understanding is little more than raw activity—like wind, fire, or rain indiscriminately affecting everything in its path. Life derives its intelligence from the consciousness behind it. A consciousness tuned to unifying love, intuitive wisdom, and trusting faith engages the animating power with these qualities uppermost in awareness, building a life experience that outpictures these qualities.

The animating principle is behind the rhythm and flow of life. Metaphors for life describe its rhythm and flow. Poems, songs, and scriptures describing the river of life resonate with us. We think of life as a journey, a dance, a roller coaster, a game, a marathon. Each of these images depicts forward, onward, upward movement, life in motion.

Moist ocean air, the temperature shift when a cloud passes over the sun, sand everywhere and in everything, diving under exhilarating waves—I relish the reliable rhythm and flow on the beach. Most summers I visit my family on Long Beach Island, a barrier island along the Jersey Shore. The beaches of my childhood are nearby, in Atlantic City and Wildwood. Although I enjoyed some spectacular beaches on Oahu in Hawaii for several years when my husband Giles and I lived there many years ago, I relish the familiar sights, sounds, and smells when "going down the shore" in New Jersey.

There is a lovely rhythm to life on the beach. High tides and low tides, and the stages between each change the experience of the water. White water crashing or sliding into the shoreline, wave after wave, hypnotizes. Waterfowl arrive, as if to the dinner bell, in the waning afternoon. You can count on hot feet in hot sand on hot days.

The rhythm of life on the edge of land is reliable, but the ocean changes, day by day. Arriving each day on the beach, you have to observe a while before jumping in to see whether the pull of the water is ferocious or gentle. You have to decide whether it is safe to stroll out or if you should swim furiously to get out beyond the breakers.

The rhythm of life within and around us is ever in motion, as well, and it changes day by day. Best to observe the moment, what it offers, and how to respond to all that is presented. Best to flow along, experiencing each new moment for what it is, sometimes getting pelted by a giant wave and sometimes bob-bing easily head above water. Tuning to the magnificent source of this life—the One Mind out of which arises unifying love, cleansing release, creative imagination, expectant faith, and all our powers—we can respond to each new movement centered and true.

The animating power of life does not merely happen *to* us. We wield the animating power. The Hebrew law "Thou shalt not kill" (Exodus 20:13) is a call not simply to refrain from ending another life. It is a call to access a *higher* life, a higher vibration of wholeness and harmony.

A forty-seven-year-old disabled veteran had been con-vinced by his medical team fifteen years earlier that he would never again walk unassisted. He believed his doctors, effec-tively strangling all hope for a healthy future, until one yoga instructor believed in his life potential. An inspiring video depicts this man asserting his life faculty by bringing his body back to life through a rigorous yoga practice. He released 140 pounds within ten months, walking and running once again ("Man Barely Able to Stand on His Own Does the Unthink-able - Amazing"). He turned the sixth commandment on its head, making it a positive principle. Thou shalt *give* life. All that you give life to lives.

The opposite of life is not death. The opposite of life is stagnation. The currency of life is divine ideas, the limitless possibilities that we either quash or set in motion. GOD doesn't give life in the way you and I give each other presents. GOD is life and you give life . . . to your dreams and intentions. Remind yourself: *I give life to my dreams. The dreams I give life to live!*

Vitality

Vitality is an aspect of our life faculty. The word *vitality* stems from its root, "vital," its two meanings applicable to our life faculty. *Vital* means "essential" or "necessary." *Vital* also means "having energy" and "the ability to thrive."

Wholeness is our true nature, our essence, our key to displaying our life faculty. Wholeness means that nothing essential is missing. We are complete, containing all necessary components. We are whole, intact, regardless of any material condition that would appear otherwise. Our wholeness is assured by virtue of the life principle that is incorruptible, immutable, and eternal. Vitality is natural to us.

Wholeness is not always obvious to us. We have to look with spiritual eyes to detect vitality, especially when someone appears to be less than whole. How do you experience Stephen Hawking, for example? The seventy-two-year-old physicist has made science accessible to the masses, introducing the world to black holes and quantum gravity via his books and public presentations. He is distinguished in the United Kingdom, his homeland, and in the United States, where he was awarded the Presidential Medal of Freedom in 2009. At the age of twenty-one, Hawking was diagnosed with a form of amyotrophic lateral sclerosis, a motor neuron disease that in most cases leads to death within a few years after diagnosis. Wheelchair-bound, almost completely paralyzed, and requiring around-the-clock care, Hawking has nonetheless successfully served in the world as a renowned physics professor, researcher, and author.

Do you view Stephen Hawking as a crippled person or a contributing cosmologist? Does his physical appearance in any way diminish his genius? Isn't Hawking 100 percent vitally alive? Could his physical condition possibly reduce his wholeness?

Wholeness is not conditional. Wholeness is a spiritual reality, a truth principle at the heart of vitalizing life. Wholeness is the fullness of life—the essence of life fulfilled.

Vitality is our capacity to thrive, to wield life energy. Fillmore taught, "The life source is spiritual energy. It is deeper and finer than electricity or human magnetism. It is composed of ideas, and {we} can turn on its current by making mental union with it" (*Keep a True Lent*, 125).

In 1977, I had been in residence at Kripalu Yoga Center for about a year and a half. I lived there with a hundred other yoga students and practitioners under the direction of our guru. Forty or so of the residents served full-time on the premises; the rest of us went to work in the community and served part-time on campus. Most of us who worked off-site longed to be asked to *stay home*.

I had quietly gone to work each weekday and come home to my seva (service)—most recently on the housekeeping team, which meant I cleaned toilets. I drew no attention to myself, truly embracing a lifestyle of inner focus. I practiced silence a lot, wearing my "In Silence" badge for days at a time around the ashram.

One Saturday morning, all residents assembled in the meditation hall after breakfast for a community meeting. We sat in one large circle on the floor. Senior residents led the session, the focus of which was for residents to speak and be heard on any subject related to our community. Our agreement was that only one person could speak at a time; everyone else was to listen wholeheartedly. One of my spiritual sisters who, like me, worked off campus and aspired to be on home staff, addressed us. She expressed feeling angry for not being recognized as having needed skills to be on home staff. She resented feeling *less than* home staff and implied that home staff thought her to be inferior. While my sister was speaking, I started shaking. I was feeling all her feelings, because they were *my* feelings, too. When she stopped and took her seat, I stood and found my voice. Even to this day I can hardly describe the energy coursing through my body as I declared, essentially, I am somebody! I want to be recognized and respected! I have talents and skills needed here! I am not a meek mouse; I am a powerful being!

When I sat down, still shaking, a senior sister stood. She looked at me, encouragingly. I will always remember her message: There you are! We have been waiting for you!

I had been holding back, hiding my light, playing it safe, keeping a low profile, living small. All the while, they were waiting for me. Within weeks I was promoted to housekeeping coordinator and a few months later asked to stay home full-time as assistant to the ashram executive director.

These words of Charles Fillmore explain my emergence at the ashram:

> When we are not manifesting life as we desire, it is because our thoughts and our conversation are not in accord with the life idea. Every time we think life, speak life, rejoice in life, we are setting free, and bringing into expression in ourselves more and more of the life idea (Jesus Christ Heals, 105).

Our vitality is expressed through our intentions. A key to our ability to bring intentions to life can be found in the first lines of the first book of the Bible, Genesis: "Then God said, 'Let there be light;' and there was light" (Genesis 4:3). "Let there be . . ." is not a request; it is a command. It is an assertion of our vitality. Let there be light, our light shining. Let me be the animation of life, the vitality of life, and the presence of life!

Presence

In principle, life is *being*, which is invisible. In form, life is existence, which is visible. The visible comes into expression from the invisible. The invisible is *presence*.

Presence is vibrational evidence of life. Omnipresence is evidence of life everywhere and in everything. We say that GOD is omnipresent or everywhere present. In keeping with our Divine Identity, we too are essentially a presence. This quality of presence is labeled, in Unity teachings, as *individuality*. Individuality means that each of us is a presence, a distinctive, unrepeatable expression of GOD, the One Mind. Individuality also means that we cannot be divided out of the One Mind. We are one with the One, and our presence displays a distinctive radiance of the One.

During meditation one morning, the background music on my iPod had faded as I went deep within. I was in the meditative state of non-awareness of my surroundings. Suddenly, my conscious mind was drawn to a base melody that was as beautiful as it was distinctive. The melody was blessing my body as well, reverberating through my toes. The base riff displayed individuality, woven into and integrally a part of the music, as well as a particular aspect of it. I equate individuality with the various streams of light emanating from a prism hung in a window. Each ray of light clearly is an essential aspect of the prism. Its presence is utterly dependent upon the prism, without which it would not exist. You and I, radiating lights of the universal Source, display a distinctive presence that is possible because we are one with it.

We recognize someone's presence, their life essence, not only in their physicality but in a quality of voice, or a feeling tone—a sense that is not merely physical but something more— one's *being*. Several months after my sister Maureen's death in 2004, I awoke in the middle of night, went to the living room, and sat on the sofa. Out of the quiet arose a thought. I don't remember the specific thought, only the quality of it. It was not the kind of thought I would think. It was humorous but caustic. I recognized immediately that it was my sister's brand of humor. It was Maureen! I didn't see her; I sensed her. Interestingly, shortly after her death I had told her, in my mind, not to make an appearance at the foot of my bed as many of my relatives have reported after loved ones' deaths. I had, however, wanted reassurance that she was whole and at peace. Knowing Maureen, a brilliant mind and a tender heart, it was perfectly fitting that she would show herself to me through an unmistakably Maureen thought.

I believe we mistake death for an ending, a failure even. We forget that our eternal being is an ever-presence. Upon death, the body decays, but our presence lives eternally. This I know. I do not know, however, how life expresses in the nonphysical realm, and I feel certain that no one cloaked in humanity can accurately describe it.

For all our hang-ups about presence separated from a human body, we experience one another's presence unattached from our body all the time. Philosopher of communication theory Marshall McLuhan emphasized, "When you are on the phone or on the air, you have no body." So true! Yet our presence is unmistakable to others. It's true when we are on social media, texting, or playing a role in a virtual life game. Those who worry about the loss of connection the next generation may suffer from reliance upon technology may do well to consider that the human system generates the same chemicals in virtual relationship as it does in embodied relationship. Our presence does not depend upon our physicality.

You wield life. Your presence, emanating from the universal Source, is filled with potential. When centered in the animating, vitalizing, and *being* nature of life, you are a powerful presence. In your spiritual presence, others may awaken to their own Divine Identity. When you stand in a moment fully alive, fully present, you may be every bit as effective as Jesus was when, in his presence, others experienced their own innate wholeness.

Meditation for Life

Breathing consciously, extending my arms out from my shoulders, I revel in aliveness. I move my life-filled body, swaying, dancing, and stretching, as a prayer of appreciation. I tune my awareness to the first chakra, the generative organs within my pelvis, the center of my life faculty. I shine the red light of life throughout my pelvis, blessing my vital organs with life. I extend life from this nucleus outward, blanketing my entire body with life nourishment.

Established in life, I appreciate the universal Source of life. That which gives life to me is creativity; therefore I give life to everything that I am creating. That which gives life to me is abundance; therefore I steady myself in abundance consciousness, knowing all things are possible and living richly. That which gives life to me is compassion; therefore I embody kindness in every thought, word, and action toward others and myself. That which gives life to me is joy; therefore I live in the delight of every moment.

My body does not give life to me. The Source of all life, that I AM. I give life to my body. I AM, my true divine nature, is movement and form, function and consciousness. I AM Divine Life.

I tune to life's power of animation. My eternal life is in perpetual motion. My capacity to understand continually expands. I am forever flowing in forward, onward, and upward ways. My vision enlarges with every divine idea I set in motion. Acquiescing to the tidal flow of life, I move and rest, retreat and extend, pause and proceed, grieve and rejoice, grasp and release.

I tune to life's power of vitality. Wholeness is my true name and nature. I am vitally alive in mind, body, and spirit. The intelligence that creates worlds is the life within me. I AM the invigorating power of divine life.

I tune to life's power of presence. I am fully present, a radiating light, and in my presence others rise to awareness of their spiritual nature.

I AM divine life, ever renewing.

I AM divine life, ever expressing.

I give life to divine ideas.

All that I give life to lives.

Practices to Cultivate Life

1. Read the Meditation for Life daily, or make an audio recording and listen to it daily. Choose one of the affirmations in the meditation to recite and contemplate.

2. Write about life in your journal. Here are some questions you might choose to reflect upon:

   - Describe the evidence you have found to support the truth that life is eternal, irrepressible, ever-renewing, and indestructible.

   - Write about the hopes and dreams of your past that you brought to life. What did you think, say, and do to give them life? What present hopes and dreams do you wish to give life to? What might you think, say, and do to give them life?

   - Hold in mind someone you know who is challenged by a medical condition. Contemplate this person as a whole being, and write about what you know of vitality. Despite evidence of frailty or disability, what is his or her contribution to you?

   - List some of the qualities that family, friends, employers, and others have found in you. Rewrite them as affirmations, claiming these qualities as ways that your presence expresses in the world. For example, for the quality "loving," you might write, "I am the presence of love."

3. Create or select a symbol for life to display where you will see it often. Here are some examples: a flower bud; an image of a fetus in utero; an original drawing, collage, or sculpture.

4. Schedule a day for renewal. Preplan this time so that you can be alone and undistracted by responsibilities or diversions. Ideally, go away from home to the woods, a park, the beach, or a quiet outdoor space, taking along your journal, nourishing food, and water. Leave behind tech devices and books. Enjoy each moment. Move or be still, as you wish. Listen to your thoughts. Drink deeply of the peace around you. Renew your life.

PART THREE

HOW TO BE THE LIGHT OF THE WORLD, MOMENT BY MOMENT

Today I will accept the truth about myself. I will arise in glory and allow the light in me to shine upon the world throughout the day.

—*A Course in Miracles*, Lesson 237

One Divine Identity, Many Powers

While reading descriptions of our twelve spiritual powers, perhaps you found that some powers overlapped others or that one power could be strengthened by another. You correctly associated the powers, because they are many aspects of the One Mind that we are capable of expressing. As you study and develop the powers, you integrate them. You discover which power you naturally call forth from within you first, because that power is uppermost in your awareness at the time. You link powers that appear related. Your integration of the powers is unique to you.

When training groups of prayer workers, I offer an example of a prayer intention and then each trainee identifies one spiritual power that could be highlighted in the prayer process. Invariably, all or most of the twelve powers are mentioned as relevant, and every one of the prayer trainees is correct.

Originator of the twelve powers described in this book, Charles Fillmore, discerned that some of the powers always go together. Love and wisdom, for example, are optimally expressed together. Fillmore linked them by associating them with the first of Jesus' disciples, John and James, sons of Zebedee. By experience, most of us know the trouble love gets into without wisdom, and the harshness of judgment without compassion. Understanding and will are also linked, both of them emanating from the prefrontal cortex involving high-level brain processes. Contemplating their relevance in any human circumstance, however, all twelve powers are linked. Their different aspects enrich and inform our reflections about our circumstances. Their varying emphases expand the range of our potential responses to our circumstances, allowing for bold, enlightening thoughts, words, and acts.

Pick any power and explore its value in the circumstances of your life. Or, reflect on the value of each of the powers available to you in each circumstance. Let's revisit the story of Robert, chapter 3, "The Light of Will." Recall that Robert had been living in a cramped studio apartment where the air conditioning and heating systems were broken. For years he had been unwilling to ask his landlord for needed repairs or consider relocating. He lived in fear of losing the little he had. Let's imagine how Robert could, and perhaps did, call upon his spiritual powers in the midst of his circumstance.

Calling upon faith, Robert perceived the truth of well-being that allayed his concerns about physical insecurity. He grappled with faith and asked repeatedly, "Is it possible I could really live in a larger, safer, and more functional apartment?" He became open to possibilities his human thinking could not conceive of. With a leap of faith, his trepidation gave way to joyful expectancy of better conditions.

Calling upon understanding, Robert began to comprehend the states of mind that had led to his conditions. For example, he recognized that he was suffering because of his attachment to the apartment that held memories of his beloved mother. Robert had an epiphany, a flash of realization in one moment after two weeks without running water. Suddenly he understood that he was *choosing* these conditions (by inaction) and could choose anew.

Calling upon will, Robert chose to be willing. He resolved to explore other possibilities for his living situation. At the third apartment viewing, he was willing to complete the application and then take the necessary steps to relocate.

Calling upon imagination, Robert stretched the limits of his ability to visualize. Having conceived of his limitations, Robert began envisioning, and speaking of, how wonderful it would be to have running water, a heater and air conditioner, and a bedroom. When Robert stood in the living room of the third apartment, he declared, "This is my new home. I can see myself here."

Calling upon zeal, Robert gave up dull resignation in favor of enthusiastically claiming his new and improved circumstances. Where in the past he would sleep on the floor to conserve space, he giddily selected colorful new bedsheets. He chose bold, brightly colored fabrics for his windows, designing his new apartment joyfully. Recently, Robert told me that every morning, he feels renewed appreciation for the beauty and comfort of his home.

Calling upon power, Robert concentrated on worthiness, on the truth of his inner ability and right to live in a safe, clean, and functional space. He worked on self-mastery to identify with the Infinite Self rather than be under the spell of human compulsions and fears.

Calling upon love, Robert recognized that his bond with his mother is eternal and that no material space could contain it. He desired his external environment to become an outer expression of the inner harmony he was choosing.

Calling upon wisdom, Robert evaluated every option consciously, noticing when his thoughts slipped into scarcity consciousness or unworthiness and counteracting them by spiritual discernment. He relied upon and cultivated intuition in the small as well as significant details of his relocation.

Calling upon strength, Robert tirelessly reestablished stability whenever he caught himself slipping into past unconscious patterns of thinking. He courageously asserted spiritual strength to complete paperwork for his new apartment, give notice to his landlord, and write his first rent check. When he had to wait a few days for confirmation that he could move into his new apartment, Robert tenaciously centered in an awareness of the essential goodness of life, of GOD, and of his intentions.

Calling upon order, Robert reflected upon the evolution of his own life experience that was leading him to accept the good that was offered him. Generosity with his time and in service have been important to Robert, and he adjusted to the knowledge that order in his life makes generosity possible. He marveled at the unfolding of his new circumstances, at people offering to assist, at furniture appearing once he'd noticed a need for it, and at every detail falling into place day by day.

Calling upon release, Robert appreciated the value of letting go of his past norms to claim a new level of living. He gently cleansed his thoughts of guilt for "abandoning" his landlord and leaving the last home he had lived in with his mother. He gave up stagnation and paralysis caused by scarcity thinking. He turned himself around, releasing many material belongings as well as interior conditions of consciousness.

Robert challenged his long-held insecurities until he started to rely upon the animating power of life. Life flowed back into Robert's thoughts and actions. He became more alive! He dreamed again, desired again, hoped again, and began again to enjoy his natural vitality. He made room in his new apartment for playing his keyboard, adopted a kitten, and befriended his neighbors. For the first time in many years, Robert welcomed friends to visit his home.

Consider an issue in your life. How could you consciously call upon each of your spiritual abilities to support your awareness and your actions? Select one or two of these items to focus on first, and begin making change today.

Wear Rose-Colored Glasses

Do you desire to generate and then sustain a positive outlook rooted in your Divine Identity?

The first time I flew in an airplane, on September 1, 1979, I was twenty-four years old, traveling from Los Angeles to Honolulu to marry Giles Whitsett, who was stationed at Hickam Air Force Base. I remember anxiously looking at other passengers and the flight crew to determine if the air turbulence was actually something going wrong—it sure felt wrong. A kind fellow traveler next to me periodically patted my forearm, reassuring me that the bumps and sounds I was experiencing were customary. I *did* relax, then, and began marveling at how tons of metal carrying hundreds of people (each row was twelve seats across in that giant jet) and all their luggage could really catch the drift that propels the massive machine skyward.

I have flown many times since then. Every time, I renew my sense of wonder about aerodynamics. I do not understand aerodynamics. It makes no sense to me that a massive jet could defy gravity. Yet an invisible principle moves the aircraft through space. I rely upon the invisible—and incomprehensible (to me) principle.

What other appearances do not make sense to our logical mind, yet we have learned we can rely upon the underlying invisible principle? That intimate relationships can endure hardships and even betrayals based upon the principle of harmonizing love? That a disease cannot repress irrepressible life?

That we can move from a high-paying job to a lower-paying job and yet feel more prosperous than ever, thanks to the principles of spiritual understanding and will? That compassion flows from individuals who have suffered through the horrors of war, wrongful imprisonment, abuse, and neglect, owing to the principles of spiritual strength and release?

Our capacity to rise above or overcome human circumstances testifies to our Divine Identity. That our hopefulness in the midst of hopeless cases is perceived in our world as uncommon, and perhaps foolish, highlights the challenge of divine audacity. It takes spiritual strength to be strong; it takes spiritual wisdom to be wise; it takes spiritual will to be willing. Activating and utilizing our spiritual capacities in the midst of a collective consciousness of listlessness and powerlessness requires audacity. Those who wear rose-colored glasses and who see the glass as half-full, often ridiculed as dreamers, are the teachers and inspirers in our world. They boldly press on despite setbacks and disappointments. They audaciously hold hope when all around them have given up. Their plucky confidence is contagious, though, and soon those who had been despairing feel uplifted and strengthened, daring again to see and bring about the good that always is.

Want to wear rose-colored glasses? Cultivate your spiritual abilities so that you can see with spiritual vision all that cannot be seen by human eyes. The following paragraphs suggest approaches to cultivating some of our twelve spiritual abilities.

Dare to dream. Dreamers are energy weavers. Dreamers change reality. Dreamers access unseen power, which is why 40 percent of the Bible is based upon dreams and visions. The root word *chalam* in Hebrew, or *hill* in Aramaic forms the basis of the English word *dream*, which relates to healing, integrating, and becoming well and strong (Errico, *Let There Be Light*, 49). Dreaming is a function of imagination, our spiritual power of conception, vision, and embodiment. Inherent in the biblical definition of dreaming is imagination's gifts of health and strength.

Within days after his elderly mother's death, when I expressed in person my condolence that I had shared earlier over the telephone, my friend gazed at me with unearthly radiance. His sorrowful tears already shed, my friend beamed with gratitude for his mother's release from a threadbare body and his certainty of her free-flowing love and light now brightening the world forevermore. My friend conceived of a reality beyond the material one; he envisioned his mother's essence in a way that assured him of perpetually sensing the love he associated with her; and his sense of peace and joy was the gift of imagination. Wearing rose-colored glasses, my friend viewed life in its wholeness, acknowledging both his humanity and his divinity.

Dare to dream of a future that has not yet manifested. The biblical proverb "Where there is no vision, the people perish" (Proverbs 29:18) highlights an urgent mandate to dream of what can be. Jesus' persistent vision of the kingdom of the heavens manifesting in earthly experience is a beautiful example of the principle of imagination at work. Despite skeptics taunting him, deplorable world conditions in his lifetime, and his followers' inability to see what he could see, Jesus kept his vision of heaven on earth in front of him, guiding his daily actions.

We, too, can be guided by a compelling vision of our Divine Identity. Affirm:

> By the power of divine imagination, I conceive of possibilities for expressing my true nature. I dwell upon these possibilities. I envision divine love, life, and wisdom pouring out from me, into the world around me, blessing and uplifting, honoring and enjoying.

Many troubling conditions in our world today are calling for the dreamers in our midst to lead us toward new possibilities. In the United States debate about gun rights, for example, we need dreamers to identify options existing in the chasm between "no one should own a gun" and "everyone is entitled to own a gun." Those who daringly wear rose-colored glasses can show us how to feed the world's hungry, provide safe environments for vulnerable populations, and rehabilitate rather than punish wrongdoers. You and I can dare to envision our preferred world of the future, contributing to the possibility of Jesus' vision of heaven on earth fulfilled.

Faithfully live as if your perceived reality is fulfilled. What we conceive through imagination, we perceive through faith. Through faith, we live as if the reality we perceive is already manifest. Visionaries King, Gandhi, and Jesus each became convinced of the invisible reality they envisioned. Each boldly persisted in painting the picture of their vision for others. In their own ways, each seemed to say to us: "I know we have not yet achieved the goal, yet every day it becomes more pressing, more possible, and more worthwhile." They fanned the flame of their vision within the hearts and minds of their followers who live today in hopeful expectancy.

Live in faithfulness to the truth underlying the conditions of your life and to your vision of the reality that you long to demonstrate in daily action. For example, if you are a long-term caregiver for a family member requiring continual attention, let faith perceive rightly the gift of this relationship to you. Let faith convince you of the truth underlying your circumstance, the truth of your, and your loved one's, wholeness; the truth of the life, love, and wisdom emanating from you even when the situation seems impossible and you feel physically exhausted. Seek the truth you cannot see with human eyes but which can clearly be perceived through spiritual vision.

Cultivate patience while in the gap between the way things are and the way things *can* be. Assert your spiritual power of order. You have within you the tremendous spiritual power to bring the consciousness needed for *improved* conditions to manifest today. It is possible to be fully present and devoted to the unfolding vision at the same time, honoring an orderly sequence of growth as found in the natural world: "first the stalk, then the head, then the full grain in the head" (Mark 4:28). Remain undaunted in the face of material conditions, sensing the organizing principle at work as conditions develop. Vigilantly observe shifting thoughts, adjusting them along the way so as to be in the world but not of it, living in the gap between the way things are and the way things *can* be.

Establish within your mind and heart a passionate commitment to fulfilling your vision. Your enthusiasm will grant an ever-present sense of urgency. Audaciously insist that the spiritual reality is the *only* reality, despite witnesses to the contrary that include your own doubts as well as reports of other people. For example, if you or your friend is given an unwanted medical diagnosis, daringly know that the only reality is divine wholeness. As you hold divine wholeness in mind, boldly select whichever treatments and remedies seem most life-supportive to you, discerned from the well of wisdom at the core of your being. Judge for yourself, not based upon others' preferences or your own fears. Trust your inner knowing about how to move forward while remaining fervently devoted to wholeness of being. Think like a whole being. Act like a whole being.

Exercise your power of release continually, gently cleansing your brain of terroristic thoughts of negativity. Guided by spiritual understanding, trust your insight that separates truth from fiction and reject false ideas. Remind yourself:

> I am spiritually intelligent. Understanding is my nature. I rely upon my powers of comprehension, realization, and insight. As understanding enlightens me, I easily release negativity.

Attend to life, your power of animation, vitality, and presence. Give life to your vision by speaking and acting as a spiritual presence that is more powerful than any physical condition. Follow Fillmore's instruction: "we are to do more than merely perceive the omnipresence of life; to fulfill the whole law of manifestation we must speak life into visibility" (*Talks on Truth*, 43).

Wearing rose-colored glasses is an active rather than passive state of mind. Living in a visionary state calls for conscious spiritual action. An idle mind becomes vulnerable to undesired ideas such as weakness, scarcity, and worthlessness, whereas a mind attentive to its spiritual abilities directs thought and action toward the reality of strength, abundance, and worthiness. Lay hold of the invisible principles that describe your Divine Identity, until they prove themselves in your experience.

Practice Makes Progress

I propose no formula and no X number of steps that, when practiced, lead to our dazzling the world with light. Even so, our capacity to be the light of the world increases with practice. Moment-by-moment attention is the way and the challenge.

Some moments are easier than others, right? How do we shine when we sense ourselves embroiled in darkness? When we are depressed? When we're feeling helpless and worried about the well-being of our loved ones? When someone close to us or we are dying? When a natural disaster wipes away an entire town and its people? When we are horrified by war and genocide?

Jesus said, "For this I was born, and for this I came into the world, to testify to the truth" (John 18:37). When times are tough and the light appears dim, it helps me to remember that I have come into this world to be the light of the world. It helps to focus attention, each day, on my spiritual abilities. It helps to study and cultivate them especially when the light appears bright so that in times of darkness the light can overcome the dark. Daily spiritual practice makes this possible. Elisabeth Kübler-Ross said it this way: "People are like stained-glass windows. They sparkle and shine when the sun is out, but when the darkness sets in, their true beauty is revealed only if there is a light from within."

Moment by moment, choice by choice, you decide whether you are only-human or you are divine. When your best friend is given a grim diagnosis, you have a choice of whether you will feel sorry for her, imagining her poor body suffering, or you will sense her Divine Identity that is life, strength, wisdom, and order, imagining her body's amazing intelligence at work.

When your flight is delayed hour after hour and you feel exhausted, you have a choice of whether to grumble and pout about your circumstances or to appreciate the gift of unscheduled downtime you can devote to reading a novel, conversing with another waiting passenger, or any of the options available in the terminal.

When your beloved dies and you are grieving, you have a choice of whether to consider yourself alone for the rest of your life or to derive strength for your future from the love that always was and always will be within you and between the two of you.

In these and other commonplace circumstances, when we call forth from within us the light of our spiritual capacities, the light uplifts and enlightens us. The light reveals the good within us and within our circumstances, which alters our experience and shifts our circumstances. Lest we worry that commonplace circumstances make for too limited an arena in which to impact the world, we can be inspired knowing that adding light right where we are is the *only* way to transform the world. Gospel accounts show that Jesus' light radiated within a one-hundred-mile radius during his lifetime, yet the effects of his light extend worldwide today. Your light can do the same.

Dare to Discover More

Mine is only one voice and one view on the infinite ways that divine light can be revealed and expressed by each bearer of the light. My reflection and study of our spiritual abilities began with Unity's Twelve Powers, and this led me to believe that I have merely scratched the surface of infinity. Limiting our spiritual powers is like trying to understand the beach by grasping one handful of sand.

A friend who practices a mystical Eastern Rite Christianity, asking about my writing of this book and knowing nothing about Unity's Twelve Powers, suggested there is a thirteenth power: laughter. Immediately upon hearing his recommendation I discounted it, thinking laughter is an action, not a power. Later, though, I thought again. Laughter reflects a consciousness of good humor, which is possible in a state of peace and joy. Is peace a power? Joy? Why would they not be?

I set out to explore how we, by way of our Divine Identity, shine divine light in the world. This is no textbook. It is a limited and incomplete treatise, a revelation for a time and by means of one unfolding consciousness. I hope you will be audacious enough to discover and develop more spiritual capacities than can be described by any one at any time.

APPRECIATION

I am overflowing with appreciation for:

Countless family, friends, and colleagues, whose audacity inspires me;

My spiritual community of the past decade, Unity Church of San Antonio, whose generosity and encouragement dazzle me;

And my longtime husband Giles Whitsett, whose love bolsters me.

RESOURCES

A Course in Miracles. Mill Valley, CA: Foundation for Inner Peace, 1975.

Beck, Martha. *Leaving the Saints: How I Lost the Mormons and Found My Faith.* New York: Broadway Books, 2006.

Branch, Taylor. "Remembering the March." *USA Weekend,* August 16–18, 2013.

Burke, Abbot George (Swami Nirmalananda Giri). "The Light Within: Section 73 of the Upanishads for Awakening." Original Christianity and Original Yoga. http://www.ocoy .org/dharma-for-christians/upanishads-for-awakening/ the-chandogya-upanishad/the-light-within.

Butterworth, Eric. *Breaking the Ten Commandments: Discover the Deeper Meaning.* Unity Village, MO: Unity Books, 2010.

———. *Discover the Power Within You: A Guide to the Unexplored Depths Within.* San Francisco: HarperOne, 1992.

Cady, H. Emilie. *Lessons in Truth.* Unity Village, MO: Unity School of Christianity, 1894.

Carter-Scott, Cherie. "Cherie Carter-Scott Quotable Quotes." http://www.goodreads.com/quotes/276475-ordinary-people-believe-only-in-the-possible-extraordinary-people-visualize.

Dossey, Larry, MD. *One Mind: How Our Individual Mind is Part of a Greater Consciousness and Why It Matters.* Carlsbad, CA: Hay House, 2013.

Douglas-Klotz, Neil. *Original Prayer: Teachings & Meditations on the Aramaic Words of Jesus—Study Guide.* Louisville, CO: Sounds True, 2000.

Errico, Rocco A. *Let There Be Light: The Seven Keys.* Camarillo, CA: DeVorss & Company, 1994.

Fillmore, Charles. *Atom-Smashing Power of Mind.* Unity Village, MO: Unity School of Christianity, 1949.

——. *Jesus Christ Heals.* Unity Village, MO: Unity School of Christianity, 1939.

——. *Keep a True Lent.* Unity Village, MO: Unity School of Christianity, 1953.

——. *Mysteries of Genesis.* Unity Village, MO: Unity School of Christianity, 1936.

——. *Mysteries of John.* Kansas City, MO: Unity School of Christianity, 1946.

——. *Talks on Truth.* Kansas City, MO: Unity Tract Society, 1942.

——. *The Twelve Powers.* Unity Village, MO: Unity Classic Library edition, 2006.

———. *The Revealing Word: A Dictionary of Metaphysical Terms.* Unity Village, MO: Unity School of Christianity, 1959.

———. *The Twelve Powers of Man.* Unity Village, MO: Unity School of Christianity, 1930.

Fillmore, Myrtle. *How to Let God Help You.* Unity Village, MO: Unity School of Christianity, 1953.

Freeman, James Dillet. *Imagination: New Thought for a New Millennium.* Unity Village, MO: Unity School of Christianity, 1998.

Fromm, Erich. *The Art of Loving.* New York: Harper & Row, 1956.

Goddard, Neville. *The Power of Awareness.* Camarillo, CA: DeVorss & Company, 1952.

Hausmann, Winifred Wilkinson. *Your God-Given Potential: Unfolding the Twelve Spiritual Powers,* revised edition. Unity Village, MO: Unity House, 1999.

Hooper, Richard. *Hymns to the Beloved: The Poetry, Prayers, and Wisdom of the Mystics.* Sedona, AZ: Sanctuary Publications, 2010.

Hyams, Joe. *Zen in the Martial Arts.* New York: Bantam, 1982.

Johnson, Barry, PhD. *Polarity Management: Identifying and Managing Unsolvable Problems.* Amherst, MA: HRD Press, 1996.

"Man Barely Able to Stand on His Own Does the Unthinkable—Amazing." Godvine. http://www.godvine.com/Man-Barely-Able-to-Stand-on-his-Own-Does-the-Unthinkable Amazing-1476.html.

Martella-Whitsett, Linda. *How to Pray Without Talking to God: Moment by Moment, Choice by Choice.* San Francisco, CA: Hampton Roads, 2011.

Maynard, Kyle. *No Excuses: The True Story of a Congenital Amputee Who Became a Champion in Wrestling and in Life.* Washington, DC: Regnery Publishing, 2005.

Moorjani, Anita. *Dying to Be Me: My Journey from Cancer, to Near Death, to True Healing.* Carlsbad, CA: Hay House, 2012.

Needleman, Jacob. *What Is GOD?* New York: Jeremy P. Tarcher/Penguin, 2011.

Peale, Norman Vincent. *The Positive Principle Today.* New York: Fawcett Columbine, 1976.

Pearmain, Elisa Davy. *Doorways to the Soul: 52 Wisdom Tales from Around the World.* Eugene, OR: Wipf and Stock, 2007.

Pearson, Carlton. *God Is Not a Christian, Nor a Jew, Muslim, Hindu . . . : God Dwells with Us, in Us, Around Us, as Us.* New York: Atria Books, 2010.

Rohr, Richard. *Immortal Diamond: The Search for the True Self.* San Francisco: Jossey-Bass, 2013.

stein, Shel. *Where the Sidewalk Ends.* New York: Harper Row, 1974.

ı. "Tao Te Ching." *Two Suns Rising: A Collection of ıgs.* Edison, NJ: Castle Books, 1996.

"The Gospel of Philip." In *The Gnostic Bible*, edited by Willis Barnstone and Marvin Meyer. Boston, MA: Shambhala, 2003.

"The Secret Book of John." In *The Gnostic Bible*, edited by Willis Barnstone and Marvin Meyer. Boston, MA: Shambhala Publications, 2003.

Williamson, Marianne. *A Return to Love: Reflections on the Principles of A Course in Miracles.* New York: Harper Collins, 1992.

Wilson, Andrew, ed. *World Scripture: A Comparative Anthology of Sacred Texts.* St. Paul, MN: Paragon House, 1995.

ABOUT THE AUTHOR

Winner of the 2011 Best Spiritual Author competition for her first book, *How to Pray Without Talking to God*, Linda Martella-Whitsett is an inspiring, respected Unity minister and spiritual teacher. Linda is the senior minister at Unity Church of San Antonio and a mentor for emerging leaders in New Thought. Her website is *ur-divine.com*.

Hampton Roads Publishing Company

. . . for the evolving human spirit

Hampton Roads Publishing Company publishes books on a variety of subjects, including spirituality, health, and other related topics.

For a copy of our latest trade catalog, call (978) 465-0504 or visit our distributor's website at *www.redwheelweiser.com.* You can also sign up for our newsletter and special offers by going to *www.redwheelweiser.com/newsletter/.*